PRAISE FOR *COLLABORATION AND CO-TEACHING FOR ENGLISH LEARNERS*

"Even with well-trained teachers and policies in place, closing the gap for English learners is often difficult because of school leaders' lack of training and background in English learner and program needs. With Collaboration and Co-Teaching for English Learners: A Leader's Guide, *Andrea Honigsfeld and Maria G. Dove provide a much-needed road map for success to school leaders. In practical fashion, professional development training is provided to assist leaders in joining forces with school personnel in order to achieve a successful and sustainable co-teaching and collaboration culture in their schools. This book is a must-read for any principal education program as well as district leadership trainings."*

—Christel Broady
Professor
Georgetown College Graduate Education

"Now that New York State requires that fifteen percent of professional development hours for all teachers and administrators be specific to the needs of ELLs, language acquisition and cultural competency, this publication could not be more timely. Thank you for facilitating the task with this book. Collaboration and co-teaching for ELLs would not be possible without the knowledge and endorsement of the administrators."

—Monica G. Chavez
Coordinator of Foreign Language & ESL
Glen Cove Schools
Glen Cove, NY

"This new book for school leaders by Honigsfeld and Dove comes at a time when many states are saying that every teacher is regarded as a teacher of ELLs. Immigrant populations are increasing not only in cities but also in suburban and rural areas. Additionally, there is a renewed emphasis on teaching academic language and content together. This leader's guide provides administrators and all supporting positions with a clear blueprint for the essential school-wide collaboration needed to be successful in these endeavors. The tools provided here are invaluable for shared curriculum development, instruction, and assessment practices for ELLs. The guide provides both essential knowledge, as well as leadership strategies and steps to achieve the goals of collaboration and co-teaching in a way that will be of great benefit to school leaders and their staff. In addition, it provides an excellent and much needed framework and encouragement for school leaders, general education teachers and ESL teachers to work more closely together toward ELL success."

—Diane Garafolo
ESL Consultant
Northern NY ESL PLC
Oswego, NY

"Whether you are a beginning supervisor or an experienced administrator, you will appreciate what you can find in Collaboration and Co-Teaching: A Leader's Guide. Honigsfeld and Dove have written an invaluable resource for instructional leaders who work with English language learners. Filled with ideas and strategies, this user-friendly guide provides school leaders with tips and tools on working collaboratively for the success of our diverse learners."

—Carol Wertheimer
Retired Principal/Educational Consultant
New York City, NY

"Collaboration is at the heart of good teaching and learning. In order for ELLs to flourish in schools, collaboration requires a school culture of rich personal relationships among teachers and children. Collaboration and Co-Teaching for English Learners: A Leader's Guide is a much needed book for school leaders across the United States and world, offering practical advice and resources for creating a collaborative approach that is important for all teachers."

—Jan Lacina
Professor of Literacy and Associate Dean of Graduate Studies
Texas Christian University
Fort Worth, TX

"In the face of a demographic imperative, Collaboration and Co-Teaching for English Learners: A Leader's Guide is an important, informative, and indispensable resource for practicing teachers, school administrators, teacher educators, and legislators of educational policy. The book should be used to prepare school leaders to engage in collaborative leadership practices that support culturally and linguistically diverse students. The contributors to this volume provide thought-provoking insights into collaborative and co-teaching strategies to meet the needs of English learners, making this book practical and relevant to a wide readership."

—Nicholas D. Hartlep
Assistant Professor of Educational Foundations
Illinois State University, College of Education

"I have found Collaboration and Co-Teaching: A Leader's Guide to be invaluable both as I train teachers in a large community-based English-as-a-new-language program, where we utilize co-teaching, and as a resource for the online professional development I facilitate for teachers around the world. I am excited to have a leader's guide accompanying the original publication and look forward to using the professional learning activities in it in my work. Honigsfeld and Dove have found a way to expand upon a great resource."

—Sally Rushmore
Managing Editor
New Teacher Advocate, Kappa Delta Pi

"Collaboration and Co-Teaching for English Learners: A Leader's Guide is a critical addition to every new and experienced educational leader's bookshelf. Schools that succeed with *increasingly diverse populations are able to leverage every asset through collaborations and partnerships. This is a guidebook by trusted experts that will help any PreK–2 program follow that path to success. The dynamic features included in the book make it equally effective as a personal resource and as material for professional development."*

—Karen N. Nemeth

Author/Consultant

Language Castle LLC

Newtown, PA

"District wide, we have used Collaboration and Co-Teaching *to strengthen the types of support that ELL specialists offer classroom teachers. Having a systematic process collaborating to create a schoolwide success model for ELL students benefits everyone in education with the reward of student achievement. We have all known for a long time that ELL students spend the majority of their time in classrooms, only some of which are rich with resources and strategies. Bringing staff together in true collaborative practices spreads those resources and strategies far and wide! Our district is looking forward to using* A Leader's Guide *as a way of strengthening our professional development and collaborative efforts towards quality instruction for English learners."*

—Heidi LaMare

Supervisor of Programs for ELL Students

Bellevue School District, WA

"Common vision, common language, common goals. Bringing administrators and staff together to create an inclusive environment and support English learners. New and seasoned administrators will benefit from the leadership practices detailed in this text."

—Judith O'Loughlin

Education Consultant

Language Matters Education Consultants LLC

San Ramon, CA

"In this book, Collaboration and Co-Teaching for English Learners: A Leader's Guide, *Honigsfeld and Dove continue sharing their experience and expertise in collaboration for English language learner success, this time focusing on school leaders. The book is written in an accessible style and can be used as a guide by school leaders to better support the kinds of collaborative practices, programs, curriculum, staff learning opportunities and school structures that make a difference in English language learner learning outcomes. The many examples from practice, together with hands-on activities and resources, will equip school leaders with real knowledge and strategies that can be implemented right away. "*

—Anne Dahlman

Professor

Department of Educational Studies K–12 and Secondary Programs

Minnesota State University

"I can't begin to explain my excitement of having Collaboration and Co-Teaching for English Learners: A Leader's Guide *to reference those schools and districts I work closely with in the implementation of co-teaching and collaboration. Finally, a tool that equips systems, leaders, and teachers with a framework that encompasses the culture of collaboration and takes it to the next level. Honigsfeld and Dove have considered all aspects of programming from novice co-teaching to more advanced collaborative systems; leading to a much needed springboard to think long term for success and sustainability of collaborative programming for English learners who are an invaluable asset to our classrooms! This book has organized critical elements of success and sustainability of collaboration for English language learners beyond traditional service delivery. The embracing of this text will certainly change capacity of those interested in beginning to be inclusive of our learners who will change how we view the world, with a more focused and equitable lens! "*

—Martina T. Wagner

English Language Supervisor/Consultant

Roseville Area Schools, MN

"Honigsfeld and Dove's Collaboration and Co-Teaching for English Learners : A Leader's Guide *text provides much needed insight and depth to this important educational topic. Based on their professional experiences, solid research, and field-vetted practices, the authors unearth to the essential issues of collaboration in co-teaching in schools.* Collaboration and Co-Teaching for English Learners *offers valuable models and suggestions to school personnel that will maximize the effectiveness of instruction, improve communication, and enhance the collegial atmosphere."*

—Kate Mastruserio Reynolds

Associate Director/Professor

Qatar University Foundation Program

"As we understand the wide diversity among English language learners today, it becomes essential for all staff to work together including principals, assistant principals, ESL teachers, classroom teachers, academic intervention specialists, content area teachers, instructional coaches and paraprofessionals to meet the academic and social needs of the English language learners in their school. Andrea Honigsfeld and Maria Dove answer seven key questions in this book on collaborative services, models, curriculum development, instruction, collaborative teaching, professional teaching and development, and leadership needed to support a collaborative approach to instruction for ELLs."

—Robin Finnan-Jones

Education Administrator

NYC Department of Education

Collaboration and Co-Teaching for English Learners

A Leader's Guide

Andrea Honigsfeld

Maria G. Dove

CORWIN
A SAGE Company

FOR INFORMATION:

Corwin

A SAGE Company

2455 Teller Road

Thousand Oaks, California 91320

(800) 233-9936

www.corwin.com

SAGE Publications Ltd.

1 Oliver's Yard

55 City Road

London EC1Y 1SP

United Kingdom

SAGE Publications India Pvt. Ltd.

B 1/I 1 Mohan Cooperative Industrial Area

Mathura Road, New Delhi 110 044

India

SAGE Publications Asia-Pacific Pte. Ltd.

3 Church Street

#10-04 Samsung Hub

Singapore 049483

Acquisitions Editor: Dan Alpert

Associate Editor: Kimberly Greenberg

Editorial Assistant: Cesar Reyes

Production Editor: Amy Schroller

Copy Editor: Jared Leighton

Typesetter: C&M Digitals (P) Ltd.

Proofreader: Jeff Bryant

Cover Designer: Michael Dubowe

Marketing Manager: Stephanie Trkay

Printed in the United States of America

A catalog record of this book is available from the Library of Congress.

ISBN 978-1-4522-4196-8

This book is printed on acid-free paper.

14 15 16 17 18 10 9 8 7 6 5 4 3 2 1

Contents

Additional materials and resources related to
Collaboration and Co-Teaching for English Learners can be found
at http://www.corwin.com/Collaborationandco-teaching.

Preface

Sometimes a foot may prove short and an inch may prove long.

—Chinese proverb

S tephanie MacIntosh, Coordinator of Federal Funds, Assessment, and ELL, Sachem Central School District, New York, reflects on her role leading a collaborative approach to services in her district:

> *As the administrator of a collaborative ESL program, I define my position as being part of a synergistic team in which I provide my teachers with the resources, time, and partnerships they need to be successful. I take the time to listen to what is said and watch what is happening in their classrooms. Most important, I trust my staff and I realize that, just like our students, we are all lifelong learners. In the poem "The Star Polisher," Leah Becks refers to her students as little stars who come to her in all shapes and sizes as she begins to "buff, polish, train and teach" them.*
>
> *I tell them that the world cannot do without them.*
>
> *I tell them they can do anything they set their minds to do.*
>
> *I tell them they can be the brightest, shiniest stars in the sky*
>
> *and the world will be a better place because of them.*
>
> *I see my role as the person who provides my teachers with their polish and cloth, gives them time to complete a task, and selects the best partner for them to work alongside. Then we work collaboratively to make our stars shine bright.*

WHY THIS BOOK?

We wrote this book to offer a leadership companion to our 2010 Corwin publication entitled *Collaboration and Co-Teaching: Strategies for English Learners*, developed primarily for general education, English as a second language (ESL), and English language development (ELD) teachers. This time, our intention is to present our readers with a ready-to-use, reader-friendly leadership guide closely aligned to the essential concepts and practices presented in the teachers' volume. Our focus is on what instructional leaders working in linguistically diverse schools need to know and do to become more inclusive, more integrated, and more collaborative in their services for the English language learner (ELL) population. We envision that this resource will offer a wide array of educational leaders—including superintendents, assistant superintendents, program directors, program coordinators, principals, assistant principals, department chairs, coaches, teacher leaders, and other school leaders—a quick read, yet one that is jam-packed with substantial information on all key aspects of creating a collaborative approach to working with ELLs.

Of the thousands of teachers who embraced the idea of collaboration for the sake of their ELLs—many reached out to us asking for a brief guide they could pass on to their leadership team on the topic of collaboration and co-teaching for ELLs. We have designed this book with their urgent request in mind and with the goal of offering immediate applicability to leadership practice.

WHAT CAN YOU FIND IN THIS BOOK?

Readers will be able to refer to this book for the following types of information:

1. Foundational knowledge on ELLs and collaborative practices that enhance the planning, delivery, and assessment of culturally and linguistically responsive instruction

2. Practical ways to implement a collaborative service delivery model for ELLs

3. Prompt, accessible answers to critical how-to questions that arise as schools design and implement collaborative practices to support ELLs

4. Access to a careful selection of vital print and online resources for additional information

5. Professional learning activities that build on the information in each chapter

HOW IS THIS BOOK ORGANIZED?

We have found that consistency and clear organization make a resource more user-friendly and accessible. With the exception of the Preface, we have organized each chapter around several recurring features that are consistent throughout the book:

- We share a different multicultural proverb from around the world in each chapter to raise awareness about the rich cultural and linguistic funds of knowledge children bring to the classroom.
- We open each chapter with an authentic quote from a school or district administrator or teacher leader to capture the essence of the chapter. (See the quote from Stephanie MacIntosh on page xii.)
- We present a short introduction to the topic of the chapter and then continue with two major sections:

  o First, we present "Essential Knowledge" necessary for understanding the different aspects of working with ELLs—evidence-based best practices for developing an integrated, collaborative service delivery system for their instruction and systemic knowledge for building capacity to bring about collaborative practices schoolwide.

  o In the second major section, "Transfer to Practice," we outline leadership strategies and recommended steps to achieve the goals of an integrated, collaborative service delivery system.

- We feature one or more short, authentic remarks from leaders to illustrate a key idea or concept we discuss. You will find these additional quotes in speech bubbles throughout the book.
- We also recognize and feature several highly regarded experts and researchers in the field by adding brief quotes from their publications. These excerpts represent relevant research findings to support a point we are making and offer further evidence. These will be found in sidebar boxes under the heading "What Research Says." (See the quote from Causton and Theoharis on page ix.)
- We include one or more practical tools, such as summary charts, checklists, rubrics, and so forth for school use.
- Each chapter ends with a section titled "Expanding Shared Knowledge and Collaborative Leadership Practices" complete with

key online resources as well as activities that extend and enhance collaborative professional learning that takes place in your school and may involve the entire school community.

What Research Says:

Causton and Theoharis (2014) summarized what leadership research has accumulated about successful practices for creating inclusive schools for students with disabilities:

1. Setting a vision

2. Developing democratic implementation plans

3. Using staff (teachers and paraprofessionals) in systematic ways to create inclusive service delivery

4. Creating and developing teams that work collaboratively to meet the range of student needs

5. Providing ongoing learning opportunities for staff

6. Monitoring and adjusting service delivery each year

7. Purposefully working to develop a climate of belonging for students and staff (p. 48)

Similar to what Causton and Theoharis (2014) discussed above, school leaders creating an integrated, collaborative service delivery for ELLs will benefit from looking to the rich research literature and decades of practitioner experience accumulated about special education inclusion. Our book integrates those findings, our own research, and practitioner knowledge about leadership and ELLs as well as evidence-based best practices in the field.

WHY NOW?

Preparing school leaders to engage in collaborative leadership practices in support of a culturally and linguistically diverse student body has never been more topical than now. The current demographic trends and future projections emphasize the growing diversity and increasing number of English learners, both new arrivals to the United States and those born in the United States. Cultural and linguistic diversity is no longer unique to big cities or urban, inner-city schools. Many rural and suburban school districts face the same challenges in addressing the needs of a multilingual student body.

Due to the No Child Left Behind (NCLB) legislation and changing demographics, ELLs are receiving increased attention at the local, state, and national level. No instructional leader in the PreK–12 school and district context can afford to remain uninformed about (a) national and state level mandates, (b) national and state learning standards for English learners, (c) cultural experiences of immigrant children and the children of immigrants, (d) how to best involve the parents and the entire community, (e) seminal and emerging research on ELLs' linguistic and academic development, (f) available ELD, ESL, and bilingual program models, (g) how to restructure schools to better meet the needs of ELLs through collaborative practices, (h) curricular choices for ELLs, and (i) best practices in instruction and assessment for ELLs.

WHAT NEXT?

This concise yet substantial guide is designed to serve as a must-have guidebook for all novice and aspiring administrators as well as for the more seasoned instructional leaders who are committed to embracing a collaborative approach to responding to ELLs' needs. However, this is only a beginning. Creating and sustaining an integrated service delivery for ELLs is a long-term commitment, requiring a bold vision, clear goal setting, creative problem solving, out-of-the-box thinking, community building, and a dedication to the collaborative process. We wish you an exciting and productive journey!

Acknowledgments

First and foremost, we would like to thank all readers of our previous volume on the topic of *Collaboration and Co-Teaching: Strategies for English Learners* (2010). Without your deep-rooted interest and commitment to collaboration for the sake of ELLs, this leadership companion book would not have been needed.

Our deepest appreciation goes to all teacher leaders, school and district administrators, instructional coaches, and preservice and inservice teacher educators who have been leading the way to support teachers with this very important work. Special thanks go to those who shared their questions and struggles, their successes and celebrations—several of whom contributed to this book with authentic reflections, words of wisdom, and real-life examples. Learning about your experiences with collaboration and co-teaching for the sake of ELLs in the field is invaluable to us as well as our readers. Thank you to

Ana Carolina Behel, Jennifer Bradshaw, Debra Cole, David Forker, Mary Beth Fortney, Josh L. Garfinkel, Craig Gfeller, Beth Jackelen, Marina Jagodzinski, Laura Lukens, Stephanie MacIntosh, Susanne Marcus, Margaret McKenzie, Dr. Christopher Miller, Julie E. Motta, Dr. JoAnne J. Negrin, Peter Olson-Skog, Mitch Pinsky, Remy Rummel, Shaeley Santiago, Dr. Steve Siciliano, Dr. Claire E. Sylvan, Richard J. Taibi, Dr. Brenda Triplett, and Dr. Martina T. Wagner.

We would also like to thank our reviewers, whose honest feedback enhanced both the planning and the writing process of this volume:

Dr. Cheryl Champ
Sewanhaka Central High School District, NY

Dr. Sheila Jefferson-Johnson
Uniondale Public Schools, NY

Mike Keany
School Leadership 2.0, NY

Stephanie MacIntosh
Sachem Public Schools, NY

Cliff Odell
Valley Stream North High School, NY

Dr. Steven Siciliano
Harrison High School, NY

Dr. Kusum Sinha
Croton-Harmon School District, NY

Richard J. Taibi
Dorothy L. Bullock School, Glassboro, NJ

Dr. Martina T. Wagner
Roseville Area Schools, MN

We cannot say enough about the unyielding support and the overwhelming confidence bestowed on us by our editor, Dan Alpert. For this and so much more, we sincerely thank you. We would also like to express our appreciation for the entire Corwin team, especially to Cesar Reyes, for their work on the manuscript preparation and production process.

Our friends and colleagues in the Division of Education at Molloy College, Rockville Centre, New York, truly exemplify the spirit of collaboration. Thank you for your continued support as we advocate for sound educational programs and practices for culturally and linguistically diverse learners. A special shout-out to Kerri Dimitrakakis, our graduate assistant, for her technical help with the manuscript.

And finally, to our families and friends who support us in our day-to-day struggles and celebrate our triumphs—we so appreciate your love, patience, and understanding.

About the Authors

Andrea Honigsfeld, EdD, is Professor in the Division of Education at Molloy College, Rockville Centre, New York. She teaches graduate education courses related to cultural and linguistic diversity, linguistics, ESL methodology, and action research. Before entering the field of teacher education, she was an English-as-a-foreign-language teacher in Hungary (Grades 5–8 and adult) and an English-as-a-second-language teacher in New York City (Grades K–3 and adult). She also taught Hungarian at New York University.

She was the recipient of a doctoral fellowship at St. John's University, New York, where she conducted research on individualized instruction and learning styles. She has published extensively on working with English language learners and providing individualized instruction based on learning style preferences. She received a Fulbright Award to lecture in Iceland in the fall of 2002. In the past twelve years, she has been presenting at conferences across the United States, Great Britain, Denmark, Sweden, the Philippines, and the United Arab Emirates. She frequently offers staff development, primarily focusing on effective differentiated strategies and collaborative practices for English-as-a-second-language and general-education teachers. She coauthored *Differentiated Instruction for At-Risk Students* (2009) and co-edited the five-volume *Breaking the Mold of Education* series (2010–2013), published by Rowman and Littlefield. She is also the co-author of *Core Instructional Routines: Go-To Structures for Effective Literacy Teaching, K–5* (2014), published by Heinemann. With Maria Dove, she co-edited *Coteaching and Other Collaborative Practices in the EFL/ESL Classroom: Rationale, Research, Reflections, and Recommendations* (2012) and co-authored *Collaboration and Co-Teaching: Strategies for English Learners* (2010), *Common Core for the Not-So-Common Learner, Grades K–5: English Language Arts Strategies* (2013), *Common Core for the Not-So-Common Learner, Grades 6–12: English Language Arts Strategies* (2013), *Beyond Core*

Expectations: A Schoolwide Framework for Serving the Not-So-Common Learner (2014)—the first three Corwin bestsellers.

 **Maria G. Dove**, **EdD,** is Associate Professor in the Division of Education at Molloy College, Rockville Centre, New York, where she teaches preservice and inservice teachers about the research and best practices for developing effective programs and school policies for English learners. Before entering the field of higher education, she worked for over thirty years as an English-as-a-second-language teacher in public school settings (Grades K–12) and in adult English language programs in Nassau County, New York.

In 2010, she received the Outstanding ESL Educator Award from New York State Teachers of English to Speakers of Other Languages (NYS TESOL). She frequently provides professional development for educators throughout the United States on the teaching of diverse students. She also serves as a mentor for new ESL teachers as well as an instructional coach for general-education teachers and literacy specialists. She has published articles and book chapters on collaborative teaching practices, instructional leadership, and collaborative coaching. With Andrea Honigsfeld, she coauthored three best-selling Corwin books, *Collaboration and Co-Teaching: Strategies for English Learners* (2010), *Common Core for the Not-So-Common Learner, Grades K–5: English Language Arts Strategies* (2013), and *Common Core for the Not-So-Common Learner, Grades 6–12: English Language Arts Strategies* (2013). Their latest volume is *Beyond Core Expectations: A Schoolwide Framework for Serving the Not-So-Common Learner* (2014). The same writing team also co-edited, *Coteaching and Other Collaborative Practices in the EFL/ESL Classroom: Rationale, Research, Reflections, and Recommendations* (2012), published by Information Age.

We dedicate this book to our respective families who are our greatest source of support in all of our endeavors: Howie, Benjamin, Jacob, and Noah; Tim, Dave, Jason, Sara, Meadow Rose, and Gavin Joseph.

We also dedicate this book to all educators who believe that collaboration for the sake of ELLs is among the most powerful tools to share.

1

Why Do Collaborative Services Make Sense for English Language Learners?

Beloved children have many names.

—Hungarian proverb

Dr. JoAnne M. Negrin, supervisor of ESL, World Languages, Bilingual Education, and Performing Arts, Vineland Public Schools, New Jersey, offers a rationale for collaboration:

> *Over the past three years, the greatest challenge and joy I have experienced is the development of a collaborative mindset between ESL teachers and subject area teachers at all levels. The journey from a "my job" vs. "your job" mindset to a collaborative one has involved a great leap of faith for many team members, but the results have been astounding. We started out having met none of our state benchmarks for ELLs for several years; however, I was able to use data to convince skeptics that what we had always done was not working. One year after*

> implementing a collaborative program, we met two and a half of the three benchmarks. That success helped me to get the remainder of the teachers on board. When I received our results, I called a "meeting," put the results on the Smartboard, and held a surprise congratulations party complete with cake! As an outcome of our collaborative program, classroom and secondary subject area teachers feel greater self-efficacy in working with ELLs. At the same time, ESL teachers feel greater self-efficacy teaching language through content. Most importantly, we have seen a corresponding increase in student achievement both on standardized tests and in the classroom. Collaboration is key to building bright student futures. (personal communication, July 22, 2014)

The influx of English language learners (ELLs) to areas of the United States that were solely English-speaking communities has set some school administrators and their fellow teachers into a tailspin. Programs, policies, curriculum, teaching assignments, and the need for additional personnel have been examined, adjusted, reexamined, and further revised to support linguistically diverse students across the country due to the arrival of new immigrant populations. Yet some school communities are struggling to find the most effective ways to address the needs of this population of learners, while others have had ELLs enrolled in their schools but have not had success with helping them achieve academically. Without a doubt, individual administrators can no longer make complex decisions for this population of students alone, and with new learning standards being adopted or developed by many states in the nation, teachers can no longer work in isolation either.

ESSENTIAL KNOWLEDGE

It is certain that ELLs will continue to constitute a growing subgroup of the K–12 student population—growing both in numbers and in diversity. On that account, no educator should enter a school building without understanding who these learners are, where they are from, what their needs are, and how to respond to those needs successfully. Therefore, the purpose of this section is to introduce some essential information to serve as a foundation for building a shared understanding about ELLs in order to create a collaborative, inclusive school culture. The knowledge we present can no longer belong to a select number of teachers or administrators—the English-as-a-second-language specialists or English language development (ELD) coordinators and directors. It is imperative that existing knowledge is shared, verified, and used. Specific knowledge of individual school ELL populations must also be co-created to support a collaborative approach to serving ELLs.

THE FOUNDATIONS OF A SHARED VISION

Who are English language learners? As educational leaders, the first questions you and your faculty will want to explore collaboratively are these: *Who are our students in this school community?* And more specifically, *Who are our English language learners and how do we best meet their needs?*

You will notice that experts vary in what characteristics they focus on as they define or categorize immigrant students or children of immigrants who are also ELLs. For example, Olsen and Jaramillo (1999) claimed these students belong to one of the following categories:

1. Accelerated college-bound immigrants

2. Students who were newly arrived in the ESL sequence

3. Underschooled

4. The long-term limited English-proficient

On the other hand, Freeman and Freeman (2002) created a modified version of these categories and concluded that there are three major groups of English language learners:

1. The newly arrived with adequate schooling

2. The newly arrived with limited formal schooling

3. The long-term English learner

In our extensive fieldwork in diverse school districts, we have noted a lot more complex variation among ELLs as well as observed the unique challenges they face based on the following factors: (a) the student's immigration status; (b) the prior schooling the student has received; (c) the level of language proficiency the student has developed in the native tongue or in any additional languages; (d) similarly, the level of literacy the student has attained in languages other than English, if any; (e) the level of language proficiency the student has developed in English so far; and (f) the challenges based on the student's learning trajectory. For an easy reference, see Table 1.1 and compare the categories established here to the subgroups you have in your own school context.

Table 1.1 Diversity Among English Language Learners

Immigration status	• Recently arrived in the U.S. under typical circumstances • Recently arrived in the U.S. as a refugee • Recently arrived in the U.S. without legal documentation • Temporarily living in the U.S./Visiting the U.S. • U.S.-born, U.S. citizen
Prior education	• Formal, grade-appropriate education in another country • Formal, grade-appropriate education in U.S. school system for a certain period of time • Limited formal, grade-appropriate education in another country • Interrupted formal, grade-appropriate education in another country • Interrupted formal, grade-appropriate education in U.S. school system
Linguistic development in language(s) other than English	• Monolingual in native language only • Bilingual in two languages other than English • Bidialectal speaking both a standard language other than English and a dialect or Creole/Patois • Multilingual in three or more languages
Status of language proficiency and literacy in language(s) other than English	• Only receptive language skills • Productive oral language skills • Limited literacy skills • Grade-level literacy skills • Any or all of the above skills in more than one language other than English
Level of English language proficiency	• *Starting-up:* Being exposed to English with no or very limited language production • *Beginning:* Demonstrating receptive and emerging productive language skills • *Developing:* Employing basic oral and written language skills with predictable error patterns • *Expanding:* Employing more advanced oral and written language skills with fewer errors • *Bridging over:* Approximating native language proficiency
Learning trajectory	• Demonstrating typical academic and linguistic developmental trajectories • Demonstrating academic and/or linguistic developmental challenges and difficulties that respond to interventions • Demonstrating academic and linguistic developmental challenges and difficulties that require special attention

NOTE: The labels for proficiency levels may vary in locally developed documents on a state-to-state basis. We used the five levels in this table based on the PreK–12 English Language Proficiency Standards published in 2006 by the international professional organization TESOL (Teachers of English to Speakers of Other Languages).

Why do all educators need to recognize the diversity of the ELL population? By highlighting the differences in Table 1.1, our goal is twofold: to help better understand the *within-group* diversity that exists among ELLs and to offer a framework to sensitize the entire school community to the varied experiences among ELLs. Educators need to resist a broad-brush approach to understanding and identifying ELLs, and they equally must resist pigeonholing them as well.

FEDERAL, STATE, AND LOCAL REGULATIONS AND COMPLIANCE

To ensure high-quality education, federal, state, and local regulations have been in place for the sake of special student subgroups. The No Child Left Behind (NCLB) Act of 2001 (Section 9101, Article 25 of Title IX) refers to a student as *limited English proficient (LEP)* if he or she has the following characteristics:

- Is between the ages of 3 and 21
- Is enrolled or preparing to enroll in an elementary school or secondary school
- Has *one* of these three profiles:

  o Was not born in the United States or speaks a native language other than English
  o Is a Native American, an Alaska Native, or a native resident of the outlying areas, and comes from an environment where a language other than English has had a significant impact on his or her level of English language proficiency
  o Is migratory, has a native language other than English, and comes from an environment where a language other than English is dominant

- Has difficulties in speaking, reading, writing, or understanding the English language and as a result is denied one of the following:

  o The ability to meet the state's proficient level of achievement on state assessments described in section 1111(b)(3) of the NCLB Act
  o The ability to successfully achieve in classrooms where the language of instruction is English
  o The opportunity to participate fully in society

While LEP continues to be the term found in official federal and state documents, many schools, teacher educators, and advocacy groups tend to use the title *English language learners* or *English learners* (ELs) to focus on the child and not the deficiency.

What Research Says:

Ballantyne, Sanderman, and Levy (2008) observed:

The term *English language learners (ELLs)* . . . refers to those students who are not yet proficient in English and who require instructional support in order to fully access academic content in their classes. ELLs may or may not have passed English language proficiency (ELP) assessments. The subset of ELLs who have not yet achieved ELP as measured by the particular assessment procedures of their state are often referred to as Limited English Proficient (LEP) students. (p. 2)

According to NCLB (2001), ELLs "will meet the same challenging state academic content and student academic achievement standards as all children are expected to meet" (§3102-2). As stated by more recent guidelines of the U.S. Department of Education, Office of Elementary and Secondary Education (2007),

Under Title I of the ESEA [Elementary and Secondary Education Act], States must include LEP students in their assessments of academic achievement in reading/language arts and mathematics, and must provide LEP students with appropriate accommodations including, to the extent practicable, assessments in the language and form most likely to yield accurate data on what LEP students know and can do in the academic content areas until they have achieved English language proficiency. States must also annually assess LEP students for their English language proficiency. (p. 3)

In an era of increased accountability, it is imperative for school leaders to become familiar with all federal, state, and local regulations.

Eligibility for services. Though federal legislation clearly defines LEP status, there is a lack of national agreement on the process of identifying, providing services for, and exiting English language learners from appropriate language support programs. Each state retains the right to determine what types of programs are deemed appropriate and made available for ELLs. Similarly, the entrance and exit criteria to be used for youngsters to receive specialized instructional services vary from state to state as well.

Nonetheless, most states use home language surveys or questionnaires and initial placement test results to determine language proficiency levels and eligibility for services. Statewide, standardized tests are administered annually to ascertain when specialized services are no longer deemed necessary and no longer are funded. As noted above, NCLB also mandates that ELLs' language proficiency development and academic achievement be monitored yearly. More recently, Linquanti and Cook (2013) were commissioned by the Council of Chief State School Officers (CCSSO) to prepare a common framework for defining ELLs in order to establish comparability and consistency across four federally funded assessment consortia. They noted that all states typically define their policies, instruments, and procedures around four key stages:

> 1) identify a student as a *potential* English learner; 2) classify (confirm/disconfirm) a student as an English learner; 3) establish an "English-language proficient" performance standard on the state/consortium English language proficiency (ELP) test against which to assess ELs' English language proficiency; and 4) reclassify a student to former-EL status through the use of multiple exit criteria. (p. 3)

In the coming years, we anticipate that more standardized policies and procedures will be developed for ELL identification as well as assessment practices. We encourage you to stay connected to and informed about what emerges and changes in the field through active participation in your state affiliate of Teachers of English to Speakers of Other Languages (TESOL, www.tesol.org) and through other professional networks.

State and national learning standards for ELLs. How can we best define measurable and comparable expectations for English learners? What English language development or proficiency benchmarks could be used to measure language acquisition progress and determine language proficiency levels? In addition to content area standards in mathematics and English language arts (ELA), many states have created their own version of English language proficiency standards also referred to as ESL or ELD standards. To further emphasize the complexity of these initiatives, some states chose the path of developing literacy-based standards closely aligned to the ELA standards, whereas others insisted that English language proficiency standards should be connected to content-based academic language development as well. (We urge you to explore your own state education department's website for most up-to-date information and details on regulations.)

In response to the standards movement and the considerable variation of ELP/ELL/ELD state-level standards that were in effect around the United States in the 1990s, a TESOL taskforce began work on a common framework and published the first national PreK–12 ESL Language Proficiency Standards in 1997. In 2002, the World-Class Instructional Design and Assessment (WIDA) Consortium received funding to initiate the development of language proficiency standards more closely aligned to the academic language needed in the four main content areas of ELA, math, science, and social studies. A new movement emerged from the original WIDA project, and to date, thirty-five states and the District of Columbia have joined the WIDA consortium, have adopted the WIDA standards (2007, 2012), and use the extensive assessment system that is closely aligned to the standards. If you are in a WIDA state, see www.wida.us for the latest initiatives and assessments, and follow the expansion of the consortium. Educators in non-WIDA states should consult both their state standards for ESL and the 2006 TESOL standards, which are closely aligned to the WIDA standards and state the five overarching goals for all ELLs as follows:

Standard 1: English language learners communicate for **social, intercultural,** and **instructional** purposes within the school setting.

Standard 2: English language learners communicate information, ideas, and concepts necessary for academic success in the area of **language arts**.

Standard 3: English language learners communicate information, ideas, and concepts necessary for academic success in the area of **mathematics**.

Standard 4: English language learners communicate information, ideas, and concepts necessary for academic success in the area of **science**.

Standard 5: English language learners communicate information, ideas, and concepts necessary for academic success in the area of **social studies**.

The Common Core State Standards. Prior to the shift toward standards-based curriculum and assessment, the focus of instruction for ELLs was, first and foremost, to develop English language proficiency. The institution of the Common Core State Standards (2010) has promoted goals for all students—including ELLs—so they are college and career ready at graduation. What do these raised expectations and intensified rigor mean for ELLs, their educators, and parents? To attain the newly defined academic goals, ELLs need specially targeted strategies, resources, and increased time to meet the standards. To this end, educational leaders must ensure that these learners receive appropriate instructional support offered through a comprehensive, collaborative service delivery system for maximum results (Dove & Honigsfeld, 2013; Honigsfeld & Dove, 2010a, 2013).

WHY A COLLABORATIVE APPROACH TO SERVICE DELIVERY IS ESSENTIAL

Developing collaborative practices in support of a culturally and linguistically diverse student body has never been more topical and urgent than now. The demographic trends and projections emphasize the growing diversity and increasing number of English learners, both new arrivals to the United States and a growing number of ELLs who are born in the United States (64%). Cultural and linguistic diversity is no longer unique to big cities or urban, inner-city schools. Many rural and suburban school districts face the same challenges of addressing the needs of a multilingual student body. According to the most current census brief, *Language Use in the United States: 2011* (Ryan, 2013), with a record number of 43.8%, California had the largest percentage of five-year or older speakers of a language other than English at home. Next came New Mexico (36.5%), Texas (34.7%), New Jersey (30.4%), New York (30.1%), Nevada (29.7%), Florida (27.6%), and finally Arizona (27%). The diversity of languages spoken in U.S. homes has also increased manifold. According to the same census brief, the top ten languages other than English spoken in the United States are Spanish, Chinese, French (combined with French Creole), Tagalog, Vietnamese, Korean, German, Russian, and Arabic. According to the U.S. Census Bureau (Ryan, 2013),

> Some languages showed remarkable growth since 1980, while others declined. The largest numeric increase was for Spanish speakers (25.9 million more in 2010 than in 1980). Vietnamese speakers had the largest percentage increase (599 percent). Eight languages more than doubled during the period, including four that had 200,000 speakers or fewer in 1980: Russian, Persian, Armenian, and Vietnamese. (p. 5)

In light of these overall demographic changes across the United States—and possibly some dramatic or ongoing population growth in your own local context—as well as the increasing demands of rigorous academic standards, we conclude that a single teacher (ELD/ESL specialist) or an isolated, fragmented ELD/ESL program cannot adequately address the needs of ELLs. When students are removed from the general education classroom community to learn, they do not develop a sense of belonging and fall behind in the curricular areas missed. Instead, a more collaborative, inclusive approach to working with ELLs is essential (Capper & Frattura, 2009; Dove & Honigsfeld, 2014; Frattura & Capper, 2007; Honigsfeld & Dove, 2010a, 2010b, 2012a; López & Iribaren, 2014; Scanlan & López, 2012; Theoharis, 2009).

We have been closely working with numerous teachers, instructional leaders, and school or district administrators in diverse school districts and observed the impact of collaborative practices on all stakeholders. We found what Elmore (2000) also noted over a decade ago: When teachers move from isolation to collaboration, "respecting, acknowledging, and capitalizing on differences in expertise" (p. 25) become possible, or even the norm. Teachers with content area expertise offer their knowledge of the subject matter content and assessments to all other teachers on staff. At the same time, ESL/ELD specialists have the opportunity to share their expertise in second-language acquisition, cross-cultural understanding, bilingualism and biculturalism, and literacy development. Building capacity and using existing talent and in-house expertise should be priorities when creating a collaborative approach to servicing ELLs.

A Leadership Voice From the Field

Susanne Marcus, ESL teacher in Great Neck Public Schools and president of NYS TESOL, discusses the importance of establishing shared goals:

> *Underlying the concept of collaboration is respect of a professional nature. Collaboration begins with shared goals for students. Once educators have these shared goals, the paths to collaboration are wide open. My colleagues and I text one another late at night, share interesting videos or readings appropriate for our students, and find ways to empower ELLs in their general content area classes by putting them in positions of "a resource person."* (personal communication, August 22, 2014)

TRANSFER TO PRACTICE

Understanding the complexity of the profile of an ELL and the regulations allow both you and all your teachers to see the immense diversity among ELLs and create a more inclusive learning environment as well as more integrated learning opportunities for them. You are likely to recognize the need to treat ELLs as individuals with unique sets of needs rather than lumping them together in a group and assigning them to uniform programs once you have tried to create English language learner profiles. Consider the rich, multifaceted information teachers will have if they use the tool in Figure 1.1. We also invite you and your staff to adapt this comprehensive list of prompts to gather the most locally needed information about ELLs. Though not required by law, no individual educational programs are

Figure 1.1 Creating an English Language Learner Profile: A Checklist for Teachers and School Administrators

Student's School History

_____ The student is newly arrived in the United States.

_____ The student has **not** had prior school experience.

_____ The student's formal education has been interrupted.

_____ The student has had poor attendance in school.

_____ The student has moved frequently.

_____ The student has **not** had time with second-language learning specialists (e.g., bilingual or ESL/ELD).

_____ The bilingual or ESL/ELD service-providing specialists have expressed concern about his or her academic progress.

_____ Other _____

Notes:

Family Background

_____ An in-depth conversation has been facilitated with the child's parents or guardians in the home language.

_____ The student is living with his or her nuclear family.

_____ The student is living with his or her extended family.

_____ The student is living with an adoptive family.

_____ The student's home has provided a rich learning environment in his or her native language (books, games, learning videos, etc.).

_____ The parents or guardians have expressed concerns regarding their child's abilities or academic progress.

_____ Child-rearing practices or family lifestyle inadvertently or otherwise may have contributed to observed student behaviors (e.g., self-help skills, student organization, daytime sleepiness, etc.).

_____ The student's family is experiencing undue stress (e.g., death in the family, loss of employment, homelessness, etc.).

_____ Other _____

(Continued)

(Continued)

Notes:

Student's Medical History

Have any of the following medical variables have affected the student's school performance?

_____ Nutrition

_____ Hearing

_____ Vision

_____ Trauma or injury

_____ Illness

_____ Other _____

Notes:

Family Culture

Consider how the student's home culture similar to that of the larger society:

_____ The roles, responsibilities, and expectations of the child within his or her family

_____ The family's goals and aspirations for their youngster

_____ The communication norms within the household (e.g., rules for communication between adults and children, language usage in the home, etc.)

_____ The English language fluency of parents, siblings, and other household members

_____ Rules for disciplining children

_____ Religious affiliation (beliefs, dietary restrictions)

_____ The traditions of the mother country (e.g., holidays)

_____ Visitation to the homeland during the school year

_____ The degree of acculturation and assimilation of the student and his or her family

_____ Other _____

Notes:

Student's Language Proficiency

_____ The student has had a bilingual screening.

_____ The student has been screened for English language services.

_____ The student's dominant language has been determined.

_____ The information obtained on the _Home Language Questionnaire_ matches the student's observed language behavior in school.

_____ The student has acquired basic interpersonal communication skills (BICS).

_____ The student has native language literacy skills.

_____ The student's behaviors are characteristic of a second-language learner.

_____ Other _____

Notes:

Student Characteristics

Learning Styles

_____ The student's learning styles have been observed and determined.

_____ The student exhibits a particular perceptual preference (auditory, visual, tactual, kinesthetic).

_____ The student's environmental, sociological, or psychological learning preferences have been considered.

_____ The student's learning style preferences have been accommodated.

_____ Other _____

(Continued)

(Continued)

Notes:

Motivation

_____ The school environment communicates respect for the student's home language and culture.

_____ The student has experienced social and/or academic success.

_____ The student or the student's family perceives education as relevant and necessary for future success.

_____ The student or the student's family perceives education as a positive tool for acculturation.

_____ Other _____

Notes:

Affective Factors

_____ The student has the ability to take risks.

_____ The student has sufficient confidence and self-esteem for learning.

_____ There is a degree of shyness that is preventing the student from verbalizing.

_____ The student is experiencing some level of anxiety in his or her new learning environment.

_____ The student has exhibited signs of learned helplessness.

_____ Other _____

Notes:

Academic Factors

_____ The student began school before the age of five.

_____ The student attended preschool.

_____ The student has developed literacy skills in the home language.

_____ The student studied English in his/her native country.

_____ The student receives or has received instruction in the native language.

_____ The student receives or has received instruction in ESL.

_____ Other _____

Notes:

Curricular Considerations

_____ The student has received adequate exposure to the curriculum.

_____ The student has received instruction in his/her dominant language.

_____ The student has needs adaptations (accommodations or modifications) of the content standards.

_____ The student participated in Response to Intervention (RTI) interventions.

_____ Instruction for the student was based on the student's instructional level.

_____ The student has had sufficient time to achieve mastery.

_____ Other _____

Notes:

needed for ELLs unless they are also designated as students with disabilities; a student-at-a-glance form may prove to be helpful in understanding and planning for individual students (see Figure 1.2).

Figure 1.2 An ELL Profile-at-a-Glance Form

Name: _____   Date: _____

Prepared by _____

Student Strengths	Student Needs

Academic Goals

Language Development Goals

Accommodations or Modifications (if necessary)

SOURCE: Adapted from Program-at-a-Glance form from Virginia Institute for Developmental Disabilities (2001).

DEVELOPING AND CARRYING OUT AN INCLUSIVE VISION AND MISSION

Exploring key ideas presented in the essential knowledge section of this chapter will also assist in developing and carrying out an inclusive vision and mission for your school and making more appropriate decisions about program development and collaborative service delivery options. Blankstein (2013) offered a powerful explanation of what a vision is:

> Whereas the mission statement reminds us why we exist, a vision paints a picture of what we can become. . . . a school's vision should guide the collective direction of its stakeholders. It should provide a compelling sense of where the school is headed and, in broad terms, what must be accomplished in the future to fulfill the school's purpose. Every decision made, every program implemented, every policy instituted, and all goals should align with this vision. (p. 94)

What will be the vision for your school that will guide all decisions, new program development choices, and policies and goals set for students and educators? We suggest the following steps to consider as you define your vision for the school.

Step 1. Develop a Shared Understanding of ELLs

The starting point for this work is a collaborative analysis of the populations and subpopulations that make up your school. We strongly suggest that this exploration and knowledge building be completed in a collaborative setting including all stakeholders. To begin, the diversity of your English learners should be determined collectively in initial faculty, grade-level, or department meetings. Frequently, teachers are aware only of the backgrounds of youngsters in their individual classrooms and may not have the school or district data to develop an overall picture of ELLs enrolled in their school community concerning their immigration status, prior schooling, or linguistic development. On the other hand, administrators often do not have up-to-date information on students' language and literacy proficiency or teachers' projections on the specific learning needs and challenges of this student population. So start a professional dialogue and never stop the discussion about who your students are and how their needs may be changing. Use Table 1.1 to review the characteristics and instructional needs of English learners in your school. Chances are the school and district demographics will continually shift to some degree and will require an ongoing conversation starting with some of the following questions:

1. Who lives in this school community? Who are our most recent arrivals that choose to live here?

2. Who is accepted in this school community, and who might feel marginalized?

3. Do we see our ELLs as limited English proficient or are we ready to emphasize the richness of culture and language English learners bring to the classroom and call them, as Fradd (1998) does and some school districts do, *language enriched pupils?*

4. What instructional, curricular, and extracurricular steps are we taking to include everyone in this community? Do we have a shared vision?

5. Who is responsible for ELLs' linguistic and academic development? What are our shared beliefs regarding what our students can do?

6. How can we create a collaborative service delivery model that allows *everyone in the school community* to take ownership of ELLs?

Step 2. Establish an Inclusive Vision and Mission

After administrators and teachers are fully aware of the specific abilities and challenges of the ELLs in their school community, language and academic goals that will lead students to mastery should be collaboratively identified. In addition, research-based approaches for teaching and student learning should be considered to determine instructional repertoires to address stated goals. Vision and mission declarations must not only focus on the desired outcomes for ELLs but also must identify the means by which ELLs can become successful. The following is a suggested, step-by-step guide to developing such an inclusive vision and mission statement:

1. Form a collaborative team that represents the school community. This team should include classroom teachers, ESL/ELD specialists, parents, and community members as well as administrators. ELL and former ELL students might also be included.

2. Establish the academic, linguistic, and social-emotional learning needs of ELLs the school community wishes to address. Collaboratively review assessment and other student data to pinpoint specific language, academic, and social issues in order to identify goals.

3. Determine ways to address the identified learning needs of ELLs. Consult experts from within and beyond the school community who have had experience teaching ELL populations and decide on priorities within the school community.

4. Identify the core values of your mission, specifically focusing on the ones that are most important for the school community and represent an inclusive vision for ELLs.

5. Draft a vision and mission statement using the above elements and collaboratively revise its contents so that it truly represents your objectives.

A Leadership Voice From the Field

Dr. Steve Siciliano, former principal of Sagamore Middle School in the Sachem Union Free School District, New York, defined his own vision as follows:

> *Since all our middle school EL students in the district are bused here, in order to service them properly, we need to have a fully functioning ESL program in the collaborative model. I wanted to see that kids who come here are not isolated but integrated and become part of the community.* (personal communication, August 29, 2014)

Step 3. Strategically Communicate the Vision

The mission statement is designed to succinctly state the shared set of values. Make sure the entire school community and the larger educational community understand what vision you have regarding high expectations and measurable outcomes for ELLs. Determine action steps the school can take to spread the word about the mission of the school and establish ways it will be enacted. Remember to communicate the vision by modeling the behaviors and attitudes you expect the entire faculty and the larger educational community to adopt. Your daily actions—ways of verbally and nonverbally communicating with everyone around you—will be a clear indication of what you believe in.

Step 4. Enact the Vision and Mission

This step might occupy a small space here, yet it will be larger than your entire school building and fill years of hard work. Start by assessing where you are as a school and identify the current state of services by creating a visual map of the services offered to students (Causton & Theoharis, 2014). Examine your school at the microlevel: What is happening in each classroom that supports an inclusive learning environment for ELLs? And at the macro-level: What is taking place in the larger context of the school and the community that supports an inclusive learning environment for ELLs? What has to change and how? Who will be responsible for which aspects of the planned change? How will it remain a truly collaborative and inclusive process? Plan strategically for a multiyear implementation of the means to reach the ideals of the vision and mission statement.

Step 5. Review and Revise Your Mission

Invite members of your school to engage in continuous reflections on how to best achieve success for ELLs. Periodically examine the school's vision and review and revise the mission statement as needed. Make sure you do it collaboratively to be as inclusive as possible.

EXPANDING SHARED KNOWLEDGE AND COLLABORATIVE LEADERSHIP PRACTICES

The following resources and collaborative professional activities are designed to support your efforts as an administrator and instructional leader to build and expand a solid knowledge base about ELLs, to develop the rationale for collaborative support for ELLs, and to initiate a collaborative schoolwide service delivery framework.

Key Resources

- If you are interested in following what the federal government is doing to support ELLs, see the Office of English Language Acquisition, Language Enhancement, and Academic Achievement for Limited English Proficient Students (OELA) website: http://www2.ed.gov/about/offices/list/oela/index.html.
- If you need information on the Common Core State Standards and how they pertain to ELLs, see http://www.colorincolorado.org/common-core and http://blog.colorincolorado.org.
- If your state is part of the WIDA consortium, follow the development of the ELP standards on http://www.wida.us/standards.
- If you want to see what is happening at the state level, regularly check your state education department's website devoted to bilingual education, English language development, or English

learners. Find an interactive map here: http://www.colorincolo rado.org/web_resources/by_state.

- o In New York State, visit http://www.p12.nysed.gov/biling.
- o In Florida, see http://www.fldoe.org/aala.
- o In Texas, see http://ritter.tea.state.tx.us/curriculum/biling.
- o In New Jersey, see http://www.state.nj.us/education/bilingual.

- If you need statistics on demographic changes and patterns of immigration in the country, visit the Department of Homeland Security at http://www.dhs.gov/ximgtn/statistics/publications/yearbook .shtm.
- If you want to encourage your staff to get to know your ELLs, explore the six tips given by Lydia Breiseth (2013) in www.colorin colorado.org/article/59117.
- If you want to learn more about your students' home culture, have your school subscribe to www.culturegram.com.
- If you wish to find out more about the countries where your students or their families came from, click on the World Factbook quick link at www.cia.gov.
- If you wish to get involved in advocacy on behalf of ELLs and bilingual students, visit the following national organizations and their state-level affiliates: www.tesol.org and www.nabe.org.

Activities for Professional Learning

1. Reflect on the value system regarding inclusive practices and ELLs shared by your school community. Try this checklist we designed to examine the core values in your school.

Developing Core Values Checklist

❏ Are you developing a set of core values collaboratively—including parents, teachers, students, and school and community leaders?

❏ Are the core values grounded in genuine respect for all students, families, and teachers?

❏ Is there consensus among stakeholders concerning the concept of equity?

❏ Are the values established focused on the learning needs of all students?

❏ Are there identified pathways for building an inclusive school culture?

❑ Are there identified pathways for moving toward cultural proficiency required for teaching diverse learners in an inclusive setting?

❑ Have you instituted a process to review the combined set of values?

SOURCE: Adapted from Dove, Honigsfeld, and Cohan (2014).

2. In *Qualities of Effective Principals*, an ASCD book published in 2008, James H. Stronge, Holly B. Richard, and Nancy Catano claim the school climate is the heart of the school. Examine your school climate by conducting focus group discussions with each stakeholder group and by exploring underlying beliefs, shared values, and the level of collaboration in your building.

3. Invite your teachers and collaborating service providers—such as social workers, guidance counselors, school psychologists, parent coordinators, or parent liaisons—to form teams and create an in-depth profile of each of your ELLs. Share these profiles with all those who come in contact with the student, make them living documents that can be annotated and expanded, and pass them along to the teachers in the new grade level at the end of the year.

4. Esteban-Guitart and Moll (2014) noted, "Children . . . create special *funds of knowledge* and *identity* for themselves through their social actions and transactions" (p. 73). The *cultural toolkits* ELLs carry with them to school are rich, complex and frequently untapped. Explore the concepts of "funds of knowledge" (Moll, Amanti, Neff, & Gonzalez, 1992) and "funds of identity" (Esteban-Guitart & Moll, 2014) with your faculty and establish ways to more fully integrate them into curricular and instructional decisions.

2 What Are Collaborative Program Models to Serve English Learners?

Four eyes see more than two eyes.

—Spanish proverb

D r. Claire E. Sylvan discusses the interdisciplinary team approach to instructing ELLs at the Internationals Network for Public Schools:

Internationals Network for Public Schools develops and supports public secondary schools and academies that serve recently arrived immigrants. With the practitioners in our schools, based on twenty years of experience, we collaboratively drew the key elements from the successful practices in our schools and concentrated them in five core principles around which we organize our work with schools. The first of these principles is "Heterogeneity and Collaboration". Because each human being is a unique individual, Internationals realizes that in any group, and therefore in any classroom, there is always diversity. Most schools attempt to eliminate this diversity by leveling students into homogeneous groups, either by linguistic proficiency, prior academic schooling, or academic achievement. Instead, Internationals Network schools choose to leverage the immense diversity by structuring collaboration among the students to work on projects that develop both their language and their academic skills. These hands-on projects require students to speak with each other and use language actively in order to collaborate to accomplish the project goals. In order for student collaboration to succeed, we have structures for teacher collaboration into our schools. In all our schools, teachers share responsibility for specific cohorts of students (about 75-100 students), that travel together to all their (major) classes (in classes of 25-30 students). At a minimum, a mathematics, science, social studies, and English/ English-as-a-Second Language teacher meet for several hours a week to discuss both the curricular projects and their students' progress. Among the team members, at least one has a background in second-language development, but all teachers understand that they share responsibility for both students academic progress as well as their linguistic development. By collaborating in interdisciplinary teams, teachers are able to leverage their own diversity, their own varied strengths, and share their individual knowledge of their students. In this way, teachers are able to focus on their students holistically, building on students' strengths; they are able to consider together the most effective ways to structure student collaboration, including their efforts to group students effectively. This broader perspective of students, derived from their collaborative discussions, as well as of their collaborative sharing of their curricula, its implementation, and their honest support for each other in discussing what has and hasn't worked makes each member of the team stronger. It makes them a powerful collaborative that can have significant impact on their students' academic achievement, linguistic growth, and their personal and social development. The interdisciplinary team structure, and the scheduled time for at least one weekly collaborative meeting for the interdisciplinary instructional team, is critically important to developing strong collaborative projects and to ensuring that students strengths are visible to all teachers and their challenges are addressed by a collaborative team. Without structures and time for collaboration built into our schools, our schools, students, and teachers would not achieve the amazing successes that they do. (personal communication, September 3, 2014)

When programs were first established for English language learners (ELLs) in K–12 schools across the United States—before No Child Left Behind (NCLB) legislation and the adoption of new rigorous academic standards—they focused instruction primarily on developing English language skills. Many of these programs were based on the research and strategies for teaching adult learners, which emphasized listening and speaking skills before teaching students to read and write. Teachers generally used a specific published series of texts developed for teaching English to ELLs, and little if any mainstream academic content entered into instruction. In turn, ELLs were rarely if ever given standardized tests until they were deemed "ready." Yet these practices kept many ELLs out of the mainstream curricula and from advancing their academic learning.

ESSENTIAL KNOWLEDGE

Considering current practices, English as a second language (ESL) or English language development (ELD) instruction rarely takes place in the framework of programs "in which students receive specific periods of instruction aimed at the development of English language skills, focusing on grammar, vocabulary, and communication rather than on academic subjects" (Ma, 2002, p. 4). In the last decade or so, K–12 ESL/ELD programs have moved beyond the constraints of systematic skills-based instruction and are being expanded to address age- and grade-appropriate general education content area standards.

linguistic competence

As early as 1988, Freeman and Freeman reported that since the beginning of the 1980s, the focus of ESL instruction has shifted from merely building linguistic competence to also addressing academic content, such as math, science, and social studies curricula. With the onset of the standards movement, this trend got amplified, only to reach new heights as the Common Core State Standards were launched in English language arts (ELA) and math in 2010. There remains a range of choices that states and local school districts have when designing a program framework that includes instruction for ELLs. They include ESL/ELD programs, structured English immersion, and bilingual education—introduced briefly below.

What Research Says:

Genesee, Lindholm-Leary, Saunders, and Christian (2005) claimed,

Research was consistent in showing that ELLs who received any specialized program (bilingual or English as a second language) were able to catch up to, and in some studies surpass, the achievement levels of their ELL and English-speaking comparison peers who were educated in English-only mainstream classrooms. (p. 375)

ENGLISH AS A SECOND LANGUAGE OR ENGLISH LANGUAGE DEVELOPMENT SERVICE DELIVERY

In an ESL or ELD program, English learners receive specially designed language and academic instruction for predetermined periods of time (typically one or two class periods a day), offered by an ESL or ELD specialist. Many state education departments offer specific guidelines for the number of minutes each ELL is entitled to receive such services per day or week.

TYPES OF ESL/ELD PROGRAMS

ESL/ELD programs may take several forms. Specialists either (a) offer language support in the general education classroom or the content area classroom in collaboration with another teacher, thus creating an inclusive setting, or (b) provide services in their own, specially equipped ESL/ELD classes.

Inclusive ESL Programs

If the ESL/ELD specialist provides instruction in the general education classroom, there are a few additional options to consider:

1. The ESL teacher and the general education teacher collaboratively plan and carry out the instruction following one of several possible co-teaching models (Honigsfeld & Dove 2008, 2010a, 2010b; Wertheimer & Honigsfeld, 2000; Zehr, 2006).

2. The ESL teacher and ELLs may be integrated into the general education teacher's lesson through differentiated instructional strategies.

3. The ESL teacher may pull ELLs aside to a learning center or a designated area in the classroom and support the general education curriculum by following the lesson conducted by the classroom teacher.

4. The ESL teacher may pull ELLs aside to a learning center or a designated area in the classroom and teach a stand-alone ESL/ELD curriculum.

Dr. Brenda Triplett, Assistant Principal, Uniondale Union Free School District, New York, explains how the integrated collaborative service delivery began in her school:

> During my first year as an administrator in a high-needs district, I was literally walking the hallways in search of our English language learners. These students had been pulled out from the general education classroom multiple times per day for academic and linguistic support services including ESL, AIS [academic intervention services] reading, AIS math, and—if classified under the special education umbrella—resource room, speech, or OT/PT [occupational therapy/physical therapy] services. It occurred to me that we were segregating students and educating them in fragmented pieces. The teachers felt just as isolated and frustrated as their students. Even more disturbing was the realization that we may have sent a powerful message to our ELLs that they are different from their monolingual peers. Thus, we may have negatively impacted their sense of self-efficacy to succeed in the general education classroom. Due to a plethora of research that supports the positive correlation between self-efficacy and student achievement, the following year, our staff embarked on a journey toward exploring collaborative teaching models. (personal communication, April 14, 2014)

Pull-Out Programs

Pull-out programs may also be referred to as self-standing or stand-alone ESL instruction. The ESL/ELD specialist either follows a specially designed curriculum that is based on the participating students' individual language and academic needs, or the specialist might develop a curriculum closely aligned with the general education curriculum. Within the pull-out setting, ELLs benefit from small group instruction and the unique adaptations to the general education curriculum that the ESL specialist is able to offer.

Self-Contained ESL Classes/Newcomer Programs/ Students With Limited or Interrupted Formal Education

To support students with limited or interrupted formal education (SLIFE), self-contained ESL classes may be created (DeCapua, Smathers, & Tang, 2009). Newcomer schools or classes may also be established in school communities with large, recent-immigrant groups. In Boyson and Short's (2003) report, 115 newcomer programs were identified at the middle and high school levels, located in thirty states at 196 school sites. More than half of these programs were established in California, New Jersey, New York, and Texas. Rance-Roney (2009) stated the benefits of these schools as ones that "provide immigrant students with intensive English-language instruction, content-area support in their native languages, and culturally responsive student and social services" (p. 35).

Structured English Immersion

According to Clark (2009), the term *structured English immersion* (SEI) was first used by Keith Baker and Adriana de Kanter (1983) "in a recommendation to schools to teach English to nonnative speakers by using program characteristics from the successful French immersion programs in Canada" (p. 43). SEI is the prevalent service delivery in California, Arizona, and Massachusetts; each state defined it slightly differently. All SEI programs require that ELLs spend a substantial portion of their day (up to four hours) focusing on structured academic language acquisition. Though heavily contested, especially in Arizona (Martinez-Wenzl, Perez, & Gandara, 2012), SEI may also be improved through collaboration. SEI providers may work together on curricular alignment, enhanced understanding of student needs, and exchange of best practices.

Bilingual Education (Transitional or Developmental)

The two main subtypes of bilingual education focus on the different outcomes of each program:

1. Transitional or early-exit bilingual education: To help students exit the bilingual classroom and enter the "English only" general education setting as appropriate

2. Maintenance, developmental, late-exit bilingual, or biliteracy education: To maintain and further enhance students' native language and literacy skills while simultaneously assuring English language proficiency and literacy development

Based on how much time students spend on each of the target languages, one-way bilingual programs (whether the transitional and maintenance, developmental, or late-exit) either follow a 90/10 or a 50/50 model. In the 90/10 model, students initially receive 90% of the instruction in their native language, which is then gradually reduced to about 50% by the fifth grade. In the 50/50 model, one or two teachers use both the native language and English for an approximately equal amount of time for instructional purposes throughout the implementation process (Bhatia & Ritchie, 2013; Brisk, 2006; May, 2008; Thomas & Collier, 2002).

Dual-Language Programs

Based on the participating student population, dual-language programs may target one or two subgroups and may be referred to as one-way (one group of students enriched both in new language and offered continued development in native language) or two-way programs (two groups of students speaking two languages as their native language). Dual-language models typically focus on enrichment for both native and nonnative speakers of English and tend to fall into one of the following two categories:

1. Minority language–dominant programs follow an instructional pattern of using the minority language for either 90% or 80% of the time.

2. Balanced programs in which the instructional time is equally divided between the minority language and English (Howard & Sugarman, 2001).

It has been recommended that either of these model programs systematically separate the two languages by day or other time schedule, subject matter, teacher, or a possible combination of these factors (Calderón & Minaya-Rowe, 2003; Cloud, Genesee, & Hamayan, 2000; Hamayan, Genesee, & Cloud, 2013). In this way, students as well as teachers have clear expectations when each language will be used in the classroom. See Table 2.1 for a comparison of the most typical ELD models.

TRANSFER TO PRACTICE

ADMINISTRATIVE DECISION MAKING ABOUT ESL/ELD AND BILINGUAL PROGRAM MODELS

While we recognize that the ultimate goal is to create an integrated collaborative service delivery system, most districts and schools are faced with the challenge of following state mandates and local policies that require them to establish an ESL/ELD program. If that is the case, the question remains: How do you select program models? The following factors each contribute to the programmatic decision-making process:

1. Federal and state mandates: All states have to follow federal regulations and provide some kind of program for ELLs under the Civil Rights Act of 1964. But in Arizona, California, and Massachusetts, structured English immersion is state-mandated over bilingual education. Some states offer ESL endorsements as an add-on to a teacher's certification area, whereas others issue stand-alone ESL certificates or licenses, which also may result in different expectations for services. Some states do not have their own legislation regarding ELL services; instead, federal laws in conjunction with locally determined approaches to ESL services must be followed.

2. Local variables:

   a. The instructional philosophy of the district or school. Are general education teachers and ESL specialists and bilingual teachers encouraged to collaborate?

   b. Number of ELLs on each grade level. Should ELLs be clustered or distributed evenly across the classes? Or is there a low-incidence of ELLs in the school that will require a consultative approach to services?

Table 2.1 Comparison of ELD Program Models, by Target Student Population and Language Goals

Program Model	Description of Model	Students Served	Grades Served	Entry Grade Level	Language Goals
ESL Pull-Out	The student is pulled out of the regular classroom for special instruction in ESL with either one-on-one or small-group instruction.	Limited and/or no English proficiency. Various languages/cultural backgrounds.	Generally used in an elementary setting.	Any grade	Fluent English proficiency
ESL Class Period	Direct teaching of English skills using second-language methodology. Students are grouped according to language proficiency.	Limited and/or no English proficiency. Various languages/cultural backgrounds.	Generally used in middle and secondary schools.	Any grade	Fluent English proficiency
Structured English Immersion	Direct teaching of English skills using second-language methodology.	Limited and/or no English proficiency. Various languages/cultural backgrounds.	All grades	Any grade	Fluent English proficiency
Sheltered Instruction or Content-Based Programs	ESL content classes are provided and followed by immersion in the English mainstream.	Limited and/or no English proficiency. Various languages/cultural backgrounds. Classes sometimes have native and nonnative speakers.	All grades, but generally used in middle and secondary schools.	Any grade	Fluent English proficiency with emphasis on academic English proficiency.

Program	Description	Student Characteristics	Setting	Grade Levels	Goal
Newcomer Programs/SLIFE Programs	First-year LEP students from various language backgrounds receive intensive ESL training the majority of the day and mainstreamed for electives.	Limited and/or no English proficiency. All recent immigrants. Various languages/ cultural backgrounds.	K–12, but generally used in secondary schools.	Mostly for students entering at the middle or high school level.	Fluent English proficiency
Transitional Bilingual Education "Early Exit"	Provides academic instruction in primary language as students learn English.	Limited and/or no English proficiency. Every student's first language is the same.	Generally used in an elementary setting.	Kindergarten, first grade, second grade	Bilingualism used to transition to all English instruction
Developmental Bilingual Education "Late Exit"	One language group being schooled through two languages.	Limited and/or no English proficiency. Every student's first language is the same.	Generally used in an elementary setting.	Kindergarten, first, or second grade. May continue for new arrivals in third, fourth, fifth, or sixth grade.	Fluency in two languages
One-Way Dual Language	One language group receiving integrated schooling through their two languages.	Limited and/or no English proficiency. Every student's first language is the same.	Generally used in an elementary setting, preferably continued into middle and secondary schools.	Kindergarten and first grade	Fluency in two languages and multicultural appreciation
Two-Way Dual Language	Two language groups receiving integrated schooling through their two languages.	Half the students' first language (L1) is English and half with limited and/or no English proficiency with same L1. All students from a variety of cultural backgrounds.	Generally used in an elementary setting, preferably continued into middle and secondary schools	Kindergarten and first grade	Fluency in two languages and multicultural appreciation

SOURCE: Adapted from Dennis (2014).

c. Number of ELLs on each grade level speaking the same native language. Is bilingual education an option or a perhaps even a state requirement—such as in New York or Wisconsin—if twenty or more students speaking the same home language are enrolled?

d. Availability of ESL/ELD support personnel. Are there highly qualified and certified ESL/ELD or bilingual teachers? Do teachers have ESL endorsements as defined by many states' regulations? Are there bilingual teaching assistants available?

e. Classroom space. Is there a separate classroom for pull-out services? Or is there a shortage of classroom space?

f. Other factors. What local variables play a role in the decision-making process?

What Works Best?

Which is the best possible program model for English learners? This question remains unanswered. Each model presented briefly above has its merits; each model has numerous documented success stories and its own share of challenges, the discussion of which goes beyond the scope of this book.

In 1985, Zigler and Weiss noted that research on program effectiveness must "go beyond the question of whether or not a program 'works' to ask *what works, for whom, how, when,* and *why*" (p. 199, emphasis added). We believe that—twenty years later—this observation may still hold true. Exemplary implementation of any of the program models discussed previously is possible and will work for some students, in some contexts. Yet we also concur with Crawford (2008) who stated that "decisions on how to teach English learners are being made not in the classroom, but in legislative chambers and voting booths; not on the basis of educational research data, but on the basis of public opinion, often passionate but rarely informed" (p. 59). In the current political context, we must not lose sight of the student. It has been documented that the most effective programs for ELLs are the outcomes of comprehensive, schoolwide efforts (August & Hakuta, 1998; McLaughlin & McLeod, 1996; Theoharis & O'Toole, 2011; Tung, Uriarte, Diez, Gagnon, & Stazesky, 2011) that are integrated and inclusive by placing the needs of ELLs, their families, and communities in a central position.

More recently, Scanlan, Frattura, Schneider, and Capper (2012) also noted, "Integrated and comprehensive service delivery [models] raise the capacity of the range of educators to accommodate student differences and do this in a manner that minimizes student isolation and curricular fragmentation" (p. 3). For this reason, we urge you to consider a collaborative approach to decision making, involving all stakeholders, and design an integrated service delivery system that works with your population of ELLs.

A Leadership Voice From the Field

Peter Olson-Skog, Assistant Superintendent, Roseville Area Schools, Minnesota, affirms the need for a collaborative approach to ESL service delivery:

> *Every time we pull out an English learner from a classroom, they lose a critical support in their language development: interaction with native English-speaking classmates. There is no doubt that they also need the support of EL teachers as well. It doesn't have to be an either/or proposition. Co-teaching provides both and should be the model wherever and whenever possible. It is clearly the most supportive structure for ELs and it simultaneously helps teachers improve their practice. The most obvious (and powerful) example I've seen is when classroom teachers observe the implementation of EL strategies through co-teaching. They replicate the strategies throughout the day whether the EL teacher is present or not.* (personal communication, August 25, 2014)

Reaching consensus about program models affords the school community a process by which pertinent information can be shared, all voices can be heard, and after everyone's ideas are considered, common ground can be reached concerning the best ELD program models for your school. For more ideas about collaborative decision making, see Table 2.2.

COLLABORATIVE DECISION MAKING ABOUT SELECTING, DESIGNING, OR IMPROVING PROGRAM MODELS

We suggest that, as administrators and instructional leaders, you make a solid commitment and take on a pronounced role of advocacy on behalf of English learners (Staehr Fenner, 2013a). Schools leaders and all members of a school community should make the best organizational, curricular, and instructional decisions based on locally defined needs as they work in collaboration. When all stakeholders are engaged in a shared decision-making process, they are more likely to come to a resolution on what ESL or bilingual program models to use for which students, how to initially pilot a new program, when to maintain and how to enhance an existing program, and why and how to revise another one. Use the Checklist for Collaborative Decision Making in Box 2.1.

Table 2.2 Who May Collaborate in Each of the Program Models?

Program Model	Essential Collaboration Team Members	Additional Collaboration Team Members
Structured English Immersion	• Grade-level teams • Core curriculum teams (language arts, math, etc.)	Assistant principal Art teachers Bilingual specialists Coaches
ESL Programs	ESL teacher with • Grade-level teams • Core curriculum teams	Department chairpersons Fellow ESL teachers Literacy specialists Mentors
Bilingual Programs	Bilingual teacher with • Grade-level teams • Core curriculum teams	Music teachers Physical education teachers Principal Psychologists
Dual-Language Programs	Core native and English language teaching team	Special education teachers Speech/language teachers Social workers Technology experts

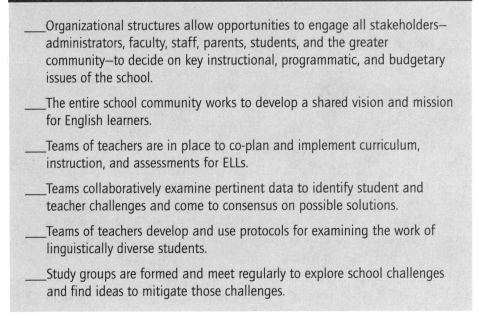

Box 2.1   A Checklist for Collaborative Decision Making

____Organizational structures allow opportunities to engage all stakeholders—administrators, faculty, staff, parents, students, and the greater community—to decide on key instructional, programmatic, and budgetary issues of the school.

____The entire school community works to develop a shared vision and mission for English learners.

____Teams of teachers are in place to co-plan and implement curriculum, instruction, and assessments for ELLs.

____Teams collaboratively examine pertinent data to identify student and teacher challenges and come to consensus on possible solutions.

____Teams of teachers develop and use protocols for examining the work of linguistically diverse students.

____Study groups are formed and meet regularly to explore school challenges and find ideas to mitigate those challenges.

> ____All teams are made aware of other teams' work through regular updates and publication of the minutes and agendas.
>
> ____All stakeholders are kept informed of schoolwide challenges and goals as they unfold.

SOURCE: Adapted from the Center for Collaborative Education (2001).

Leadership Voices From the Field

Lisa Wittek, ESL teacher at French Road Elementary School, Rochester, New York, and her colleagues Beth Jackelen and Marina Jagodzinski, both fourth-grade teachers, exemplify a team approach to serving ELLs and explain what their collaboration looks like:

> *Our fourth-grade ELLs work with a team of three teachers who provide them with rich opportunities for acquiring English in multiple ways. My colleagues, Beth Jackelen and Marina Jagodzinski, are teaching partners on the fourth-grade team—collaboration was already built in, and it helped from the onset. Adding myself as the ESL specialist further strengthened this unit. We planned in and out of school, utilizing text messages, e-mail, Pinterest boards, attending professional development workshops together, as well as "traditional" face-to-face planning. Marina, a veteran teacher, was initially apprehensive about working with ELLs. I've collaborated with Beth for several years, and we encouraged Marina to join us. Marina and I were part of a grant for all teachers of ELLs through the University of Rochester. Through the grant, we purchased iPads that traveled between the students' homerooms and my stand-alone ESL program, allowing students to work on projects in multiple settings. I pretaught concepts and vocabulary to our students as well as provided scaffolded lessons and enrichment opportunities to deepen their understanding. Our shared kids were empowered, engaged, and able to teach concepts to their non-ELL peers. My colleagues have embraced our ELLs, allowed them to be "experts" in class, and provided them with multiple ways to "show what they know." When I push into my colleagues' classrooms and teach lessons with the assistance of our ELLs, we offer them more opportunities for learning, sharing, and growing.* (personal communication, July 17, 2014)

INFUSING COLLABORATIVE PRACTICES ACROSS ALL EXISTING PROGRAMS

Formal collaborative practices to support ELLs' linguistic and academic development may have a direct instructional or noninstructional focus and be infused throughout an entire school day in a substantive way. Instructional activities include (1) joint planning, (2) curriculum mapping and alignment, (3) parallel teaching, (4) co-developing instructional materials, (5) collaborative assessment of student work, and (6) co-teaching. At the same time, noninstructional activities may include (1) joint professional development, (2) teacher research, (3) preparing for and conducting joint parent-teacher conferences, and (4) planning, facilitating, or participating in other extracurricular activities. Table 2.3 gives you a snapshot of these collaborative practices. For a more detailed discussion of each of these activities, see our companion publication *Collaboration and Co-Teaching: Strategies for English Learners* (Honigsfeld & Dove, 2010a).

Table 2.3 Opportunities for Instructional Collaborations

Collaborative Practices Aligned to Instruction	Goals	Look-Fors
Joint planning	• To establish attainable yet rigorous learning targets • To share instructional routines and strategies • To align instructional content • To design appropriate formative and summative assessment measures	Daily lesson plans and unit plans reflective of the following: • Language and content objectives • Knowledge of diverse ELLs' needs • Strategically selected instructional accommodations and accelerations • Differentiated instruction according to students' academic and linguistic abilities
Curriculum mapping and alignment	• To plan and align instruction for a longer period of time • To have an overall guide for joint planning, parallel teaching, and co-instruction	• Rigor, relevance, and research-informed approaches infused into the curriculum • Instructional intensity in the planned and taught curriculum for ELLs
Parallel teaching	• To accelerate ELLs' knowledge and understanding of mainstream curricula	• Coordination and sharing of lesson goals and objectives

Collaborative Practices Aligned to Instruction	Goals	Look-Fors
	• To ensure that what happens during ELD/ESL lessons parallels general class instruction	• Established content for the ESL teacher to pre-teach or re-teach
Co-developing instructional materials	• To scaffold instructional materials • To select essential materials that support accelerated learning	• Differentiated, tiered, teacher-made resources • Chunking of complex materials or tasks into manageable segments • Selection of essential learning tools
Collaborative assessment of student work	• To jointly examine ELLs' language and academic performance • To analyze student data and identify areas that need improvement or targeted intervention	• Shared formative and summative assessment measures • Co-developed assessment tasks • Joint goal setting for ELLs using assessment data
Co-teaching	• To co-deliver instruction through differentiated instruction • To use various models of instruction to establish equity between co-teaching partners	• Co-equal partnership • Shared ownership for learning • Engagement in the entire collaborative instructional cycle
Joint professional learning (See more on this in Chapter 6 addressing professional development.)	• To enhance pedagogical knowledge, skills, and dispositions about ELLs • To established a shared understanding about ELLs' needs, best practices, and effective strategies • To explore new and emerging directions in ELD/ESL education	• Sustained engagement in learning with colleagues • Application of new learning to teaching • Reflection of new learning • Opportunities to showcase new learning

Collaboration is a twenty-first century skill and a much-neglected professional opportunity for job-embedded teacher learning. It needs to be championed, nurtured, and refined over time, and to become a well-established, routine part of how the school community operates.

What Research Says:

Martinez-Wenzl et al. (2012) concluded that

the research is consistent in finding that it takes students significantly longer than a year or two to become proficient in academic language. As a result, students who are in mainstream classes before they have developed the requisite language skills to fully participate are not in fact being afforded equal access to the curriculum. Nor are students being provided with an adequate education if they are denied grade level instruction in academic content while they learn English. Moreover, the research is now clear and overwhelming that trading off the instruction of academic content by focusing on instruction about English does not result in superior outcomes even for English acquisition. (pp. 25–26)

EXPANDING SHARED KNOWLEDGE AND COLLABORATIVE LEADERSHIP PRACTICES

The following resources and collaborative professional activities are designed to support your efforts as an administrator and instructional leader to build and expand a solid knowledge base about ESL/ELD programs and to develop an integrated, collaborative service delivery system.

Key Resources

If you want to stay up-to-date on what the most prominent professional organizations or government agencies are saying related to ESL/ELD program models and program implementation issues, visit these sites:

- Teachers of English to Speakers of Other Languages: www.tesol.org
- National Clearinghouse for English Language Acquisition: www.ncela.gwu.edu
- U.S. Department of Education, Office of English Language Acquisition: www.ed.gov/offices/OELA
- WestEd: www.wested.org/area_of_work/english-language-learners/
- Center for Applied Linguistics: www.cal.org/

- ¡Colorín Colorado!: www.colorincolorado.org/educators/back ground/programs/

Activities for Professional Learning

1. In the introduction of their edited volume, Schatz and Wilkinson (2010) emphasized that school leaders and administrators must make creating a collaborative school culture their priority and listed encouraging teamwork and cross-disciplinary collaboration among school staff as the number-one goal. They stated the following:

Principals need to have the teaching and learning of ELLs as a priority within the school community: They need to nurture the school community with specific actions, such as scheduling time and opportunities for regular classroom teachers to collaborate with ESL teachers in comparing teaching strategies, in reviewing the progress of ELLs in their classes, and in identifying key resources that can be applied to the education of ELLs. Moreover, in their roles as instructional leaders, principals must identify instructional techniques to use when working with ELLs, such as scaffolded instruction, targeted vocabulary development, connections to student experiences, student-to-student interaction, and the use of supplementary culturally relevant materials. In short, principals need to support instruction that builds language lessons into content areas and integrates L1 and L2 in meaningful ways in the classroom. (pp. 18–19)

With your faculty, collaboratively examine (a) what has been done to encourage teamwork and cross-disciplinary collaboration as outlined in this quote and (b) what should be done to further enhance such teamwork and collaboration in your school. Take a full inventory and prioritize the plans for improvement.

2. Invite teachers to join a task force or subcommittee for each of the program models currently implemented in your school. Examine the perceived benefits and challenges the school community faces while implementing each model. Identify specific ways to address the challenges found in each program model.

3. Although a recent study by Elfers and Stritikus (2014) focuses primarily on general education teachers' needs to better serve ELLs, their research is comprehensive, the findings are compelling, and the recommendations demand a closer look. Examine the findings

of the study regarding the types of leadership actions they documented that support classroom teachers' work with ELLs. Consider which of the actions presented in the textbox are transferable to your own school or district context and discuss steps you would need to take to implement them.

School leaders successful with ELLs accomplish the following:

1. Focus on high-quality instruction.

Leaders directly engage in teaching and learning initiatives.

Professional development targets classroom teachers.

Instructional decisions take into account the teachers of ELLs.

Leaders align, integrate, and coordinate supports for teachers.

2. Blend district- and school-level initiatives.

Focus on district workforce development practices.

Create opportunities for staff to work collaboratively.

Leverage local expertise in schools and communities to serve ELLs.

Engage in strong two-way communication between school and district leaders.

3. Communicate a compelling rationale.

Make instruction of ELLs a priority.

Encourage staff responsibility to serve ELLs.

Focus on instructional practices to serve diverse learners.

4. Differentiate support systems at elementary and secondary levels.

Prioritize supports for those serving the largest number of ELLs.

Value students' language and culture in instruction.

Model ways that instructional leaders can serve ELLs.

5. Use data for instructional improvement.

Support data-based discussions of individual student progress.

Use data to identify areas for improvement, shape professional development, and support a culture of learning.

SOURCE: Adapted from Elfers and Stritikus (2014).

3 How Do You Support Shared Curriculum Development and Implementation for the Sake of ELLs?

One person's plans are short, but those made by two people are long.

—Chinese proverb

Julie Motta, Assistant Superintendent, East Providence School District, Rhode Island, discusses the curriculum mapping initiative:

> *In implementing the Common Core State Standards (CCSS) and related curriculum with our ELLs in my district, I knew it was imperative to find the time to have my ESL teachers work together to have the opportunity to "dissect" the CCSS aligned ELA curriculum units that had been written for the general population without our ELLs in mind. In keeping this work focused and manageable, I created a unit*

template* that allowed my teachers to produce an ESL/CCSS curriculum tool that they could pick up and use relatively easily with our students. They spent time on linking the content standards with our English language development standards, writing essential questions in accessible language, creating model performance indicators that would allow students to showcase the language and the content knowledge they had acquired. Most importantly, they collaborated on ESL teaching strategies that would accelerate academic language and content learning in the curriculum units. It was a joy to witness and listen to the high-quality professional discussions that took place as my ESL teachers shared the "tricks of the trade" that they possessed both individually and collectively to ensure that the necessary scaffolding was put into place to ensure that students were successful with rigorous concepts, complex texts and high-level academic vocabulary and intricate writing activities. Working together, they used their talents and deep pedagogical and linguistic knowledge to write curriculum aligned to the CCSS that ELLs could be highly successful in learning. (personal communication, June 16, 2014)

Most educators are familiar with different types of written curricula—be it English language arts (ELA), mathematics, social studies, science, or some other school subject. Generally speaking, each curriculum identifies the overall subject matter, academic standards, learning objectives, related assessments, and instructional resources necessary for students to gain content knowledge and skills. Often, exemplary curriculum guides show a progression for learning that occurs across grade levels, identify pathways for interdisciplinary approaches to teaching, and affirm the need for periodic examination and revision. However, if you searched for examples of typical curriculum guides in any subject that include comprehensive, fully integrated information for teaching ELLs (English language learners), you would be hard pressed to find any at all.

ESSENTIAL KNOWLEDGE

All too often, curriculum guides have "add-on" information with a designated special section where instruction for ELLs is addressed in general terms, including at times broad-based strategies and recommendations. Yet they offer little guidance to teachers as to how to teach specific content or skills, modify assessments, clearly enhance instruction, or identify adequate resources for teaching ELLs. With so many states adopting new learning standards, curricular revisions are taking

---

* See https://ccweta.files.wordpress.com/2014/06/final-template-for-curriculum-work1.pdf

place in just about every school district. For this reason, it is critical that instructional leaders consider the impact curricular revisions will have on their population of ELLs.

STANDARDS-BASED CURRICULUM DEVELOPMENT

Heidi Hayes Jacobs (2010) cautioned that "running schools and using curriculum on a constant *replay* button no longer works. It is critical that we become active researchers and developers of innovations and new directions" (p. 8). For this reason, school leaders need to take an enterprising review of the way in which curriculum development is addressed. Therefore, we encourage you to create innovative curricula that are inclusive of English learners. One critical first step prior to engaging the entire staff in collaborative, standards-based curriculum work is to facilitate critical reflections and honest conversations centered on the following broad-based questions:

- What are the new directions for standards-based curriculum development and to what degree do they include ELLs?
- How can we venture into innovations that stem from sound research and evidence-based practices when standards are often perceived to be—and are frequently connected to—something that is standardized such as high-stakes testing?
- What do the new core standards in ELA, math, and science mean for all learners?
- What is the latest evidence-based and research-informed professional knowledge your faculty shares?
- How do you collectively nurture the courage in teachers to be inquisitive, innovative, and reflective in their day-to-day work with curriculum design, adaptation, and implementation?

In light of the standards movement—be it the Common Core State Standards, the New Generation Science Standards, or your newly developed college- and career-readiness state standards—curriculum development will require the combination of rigor, relevance, and research-based best practices (Daggett, 2012; Dove & Honigsfeld, 2013; Dove, Honigsfeld, & Cohan, 2014; Honigsfeld & Dove, 2013) as well as ongoing systemic collaboration among educators. Carefully crafted curricula will prepare students for the unfolding future and lifelong learning rather than merely reinforcing knowledge and skills for the present or the past.

What Research Says:

Valdés, Kibler, and Walqui (2014) observed,

> The curriculum must be implemented in a manner that provides the necessary content to address students' linguistic needs and facilitate their participation in inclusive, Standards-based classrooms as soon as possible. The collaboration of both ESL and content-area teachers is necessary at all levels to ensure that beginning ELLs have as much access to the curriculum as their English and home language proficiencies will allow, but this cooperation is particularly essential at earlier levels of proficiency. (p. 16)

A mantra you must have heard—and most likely repeated—many times remains true: The standards are not the curriculum; they identify the desirable goals and end-of-year or end-of-course expectations. The curriculum will need to translate those goals into essential learning outcomes—what the students need to *know, understand,* and be able to *do* (KUDs) (Erickson, 2006; Wiggins & McTighe, 2005). The curriculum should also contain a scope and sequence of the content, the choice of resources and expected progressions (Hattie, 2012), and what formative and summative measures will indicate attainment of goals (Jung & Guskey, 2012).

ENGLISH LANGUAGE ARTS AND CONTENT AREA CURRICULA FOR ELLS

Acquiring the K–12 core curriculum is a necessity for success in school and beyond. In order to develop an advocacy framework, Staehr Fenner (2013a) offered a series of powerful reflection and self-evaluation questions for school and district administrators, one of which probed whether or not all ELLs have "access to a challenging, high-quality and developmentally appropriate curriculum aligned to the state's standards within and across content areas" (p. 87). Ainsworth (2010) also proposed the creation of a rigorous curriculum in each content area and defined it as

> an inclusive set of intentionally aligned components—clear learning outcomes with matching assessments, engaging learning experiences, and instructional strategies—organized into sequenced units of study that serve as both the detailed road map and the high-quality delivery system for ensuring that all students achieve the desired end: the attainment of their designated grade- or course-specific standards within a particular content area. (Kindle Locations, 479–483)

The grade-appropriate curriculum serving as a road map in ELA and all content areas must be translated into meaningful instructional experiences for ELLs through curricular *adaptations* and *acceleration* using the expertise of the ESL/ELD (English language development) team as leverage. Adaptations may take the form of accommodations—offering access to the grade-level curriculum without altering the standards—or modifications—fundamental changes to the grade-level expectations when the standards are not attainable by the ELL due to disabilities or other confounding variables. Rollins (2014) also noted,

> a crucial aspect of the acceleration model is putting key prior knowledge into place so that students have something to connect new information to. Rather than focus on everything students don't know about the concept, however, the core and acceleration teachers collaboratively and thoughtfully select the specific prior knowledge that will best help students grasp the upcoming standard. (pp. 6–7)

Accelerating the curriculum moves away from the notion of remediation; instead, it allows for developing relevant, thinking-oriented curricula and collaborative, low-stakes practice while also offering foundational skills building and intentional support for students' social-emotional needs (Hern, 2013). Walqui and van Lier (2010) suggested five design factors to be included in a quality curriculum for ELLs:

1. Setting long-term goals and benchmarks

2. Using a problem-based approach that includes interrelated lessons with real-life applications

3. Creating a spiraling progression that includes necessary pre-teaching and re-teaching

4. Making the subject matter relevant to the present lives and future goals of the students and their communities

5. Building on students' lived experiences and connecting to the students' funds of knowledge (p. 99)

Additional curriculum design decisions include (a) tiered goals, (b) culturally responsive instructional resources, (c) scaffolding the learning experiences, and (d) applying appropriate formative and summative assessment practices.

Tiered goals. It is best to recognize ELLs as a heterogeneous group of youngsters, each with their own levels of literacy, academic achievement, and English language proficiency. For this reason, supporting these students through the use of tiered goals can establish a pathway for each of them to meet academic benchmarks through intermittent steps developed for individual learners.

Culturally responsive resources. To meet this criterion, curriculum design must move beyond the token cultural holiday or historical person study from select ethnic groups and incorporate the lived experiences of students from the various cultural groups represented in the school. It is essential that students be able to see their lives reflected in what is being taught.

Scaffolded learning experiences. Scaffolding provides students with smaller bits of information supported by the use of graphic organizers, guiding questions, small-group activities, and so on. Its practice maintains the intensity and rigor of instruction, yet provides smaller doses of information for students to examine, analyze, and acquire in a given time.

Appropriate formative and summative assessments. As educators, the assessment policies and practices mandated by federal, state, and local governments bind us all. However, these assessment directives should not preclude what we know as sound formative and summative evaluative practices to gain accurate knowledge of what students know and are able to do at various stages of their developing academic and language proficiency.

A Leadership Voice From the Field

Laura Lukens, ELL Coordinator, North Kansas City Schools, Kansas City, Missouri, discusses the shifting role of ESL teachers in the context of standards-based education:

Collaboration between ELL and classroom teachers is imperative if ELLs are to meet the challenges of learning language and grade-level content at the same time. The days of ELL teachers bringing small groups of students to their rooms, closing the doors, and teaching language in isolation are over. With higher standards and more rigorous assessments, the role of the ELL teacher has shifted to that of consultant and collaborator, partnering with content and classroom teachers to ensure that "our" students become successful, independent learners. Empowering ELL teachers and classroom teachers is our role as leaders, ensuring that they have the time and resources they need to collaborate effectively. (personal communication, August 27, 2014)

LOCALLY DEVELOPED AND COMMERCIALLY AVAILABLE ESL CURRICULA

Curricula for ELD or ESL programs may come readily available from leading publishers of such materials or may be developed locally. Frequently, the taught curriculum turns out to be a unique combination of commercially available programs and teacher-made resources. The critical point is to empower and engage your instructional team to collaboratively decide and develop the ESL curriculum based on locally determined needs and circumstances. These variables include but are not limited to the size and composition of the ELL population, the levels of language proficiency and academic readiness represented among ELLs, students' cultural backgrounds and experiences, themes and learning targets identified in the units of study, and the academic language of the overall taught curriculum to the general student body.

What are some curricular options you and your district or school could consider?

1. An integrated ESL curriculum based on English language development and academic content standards

2. A stand-alone ESL curriculum following a locally developed progression of language and literacy skills

3. A stand-alone ESL curriculum following a statewide ESL or ELA curriculum framework

4. A stand-alone ESL curriculum based on a commercially available ESL program

5. A flexible curriculum framework using a combination of the above.

Rather than strictly defining the ESL curriculum one way or another, consider a more flexible approach. Depending on students' language proficiency levels and other individual variables depicted in Table 1.1, some ELLs (such as students with interrupted formal education) will need a core curriculum with foundational language and content goals, whereas newly arrived ELLs with strong schooling background will benefit from a more intensive, accelerated curriculum design (Calderón, Slavin, & Sánchez, 2011). As Lynne Sacks (2014) noted in a recent blog post, what must be remembered is this:

Administrators and teachers need to re-examine ELL placement, shifting their focus from just teaching ELLs English to ensuring

ELLs have full access to the academic curriculum. Next is a curriculum designed to foster deep engagement, creativity, and mastery taught by teachers who have been well trained to do those things. Finally, teachers must provide language support tailored to students' developing English skill levels. This means, for example, teaching relevant vocabulary explicitly and more than once, modeling writing forms for different subjects, and providing frameworks as well as time and patience for students to discuss ideas in a language they are still learning. (para 7)

The shift to high expectations paired with high levels of support (Walqui & van Lier, 2010) allows for rigorous curriculum implementation across the grades. See more on instructional practices in Chapter 4.

TRANSFER TO PRACTICE

Curriculum Mapping and Alignment

The initial approach to ensuring ELLs are making progress toward meeting the grade-appropriate content curricular goals and their language development goals is curriculum mapping and alignment. These organizational methods are essential to ensuring that ELLs have access to the general academic curricula as well as appropriate English language instruction. Let's take a closer look at the practical applications of each.

Curriculum mapping. Jacobs (1997, 2010), Udelhofen (2005), and others agree that curriculum mapping is an effective procedure for collecting data about the taught curriculum in a school or district using a yearly or monthly calendar as the framework. Once such overviews of students' actual learning experiences are created in the various content areas, teachers engage in a dialogue to ensure alignment and explore possible misalignments of essential knowledge and skills taught in the general education and ESL curricula. As Jacobs (2010) noted,

An active and deliberate examination of the curriculum is the essence of mapping. Mapping is a verb, an action to be carried out by faculties as they breathe life into the curriculum. The goal is to formally upgrade all three fundamental elements of the curriculum [content, skills, and assessment] and reconsider the essential questions that bind and focus on them. (pp. 21–22)

Curriculum planning, mapping, and alignment among ESL professionals are receiving increasing attention due to the rigor of the new content standards and the increased need for collaboration among all educators. In Table 3.1, we summarize what is targeted and what is to be accomplished when curriculum planning is the focus of collaborative efforts for the sake of ELLs.

Most maps reveal four types of information: the content (essential knowledge taught), the processes and skills used to teach the content, the assessment tools, and the key resources used. The year-at-a-glance template we like to use allows for differentiation for beginner, intermediate, and advanced ELLs (see Figure 3.1). Similarly, curriculum mapping may focus on shorter time periods, such as a semester or a unit at a time.

Curriculum mapping may be carried out both by looking back (backward mapping) and looking ahead (forward mapping). Table 3.2 offers a useful summary to reflect on the advantages and disadvantages of different types of curriculum mapping from the ESL perspective.

Udelhofen (2005) identified curriculum mapping as a process "that is respectful of the knowledge of every teacher, encourages collaboration and reflection, and is sensitive to the complexities of student learning and the teaching profession" (p. 3). The most prevalent feature of curriculum mapping lies in its flexibility, since the process allows for

Table 3.1 What Is ESL Curriculum Planning?

What Is Targeted?	What Is to Be Accomplished?
Entire district	To establish common goals and a common curriculum framework from prekindergarten to high school graduation; the focus is on curriculum mandates, curriculum continuity, and meeting state standards and state regulations
Whole school	To plan coordinated instruction based on locally defined, broad-based outcomes
Multiple grades	To plan a multigrade scope and sequence of target content area to meet established district and school goals and establish opportunities for curriculum acceleration
Grade level	To plan learning experiences within the multigrade scope and sequence of the content
Class or group	To establish learning targets and plan scaffolded and differentiated learning activities, resources, and assessment tools
Individual	To plan individualized instruction for students by accelerating and/or adapting curricula using appropriate accommodations and modifications

Figure 3.1 Year-at-a-Glance ESL Curriculum-Mapping Template

GRADE: _____ TEACHER: _____

Month	Essential Questions	LANGUAGE SKILLS CONTENT GOALS			Resources	Assessment
		BEGINNER	INTERMEDIATE	ADVANCED		

Table 3.2 Backward (Journal) Mapping Versus Forward (Projection) Mapping		
Initial Mapping Format	**Advantages**	**Disadvantages**
Backward mapping *(Sometimes referred to as journal or diary mapping)*	• This type of mapping is less time-intensive; it requires a small amount of time on a regular basis to record the ESL and general education content, language skills, and assessments taught each month. • When various levels of language proficiency are considered, this type of mapping allows for a more accurate account of what was actually taught to various groups of ELLs.	• It slows the completion of the initial mapping cycle, as teachers cannot proceed to the editing step until maps are completed. • The next steps probably would not occur until the beginning of the subsequent school year. • The curriculum mapping process can lose momentum. • Monthly check-ins must occur with each teacher to keep abreast of everyone's progress.
Forward mapping *(Sometimes referred to as projection mapping)*	• The initial curriculum maps are completed within a short time frame, enabling teachers to move to the next steps of mapping much faster. • If a district allocates the appropriate amount of time, the initial cycle of mapping can be completed in one academic year.	• It is more time intensive. • Some teachers may have difficulty projecting future teaching. • It is troublesome for teachers who wish to document their differentiated maps for the three language proficiency levels.

SOURCE: Adapted from Udelhofen (2005).

addressing the changing curriculum needs of school districts. In addition, it invites active participation from all teachers and depends on their expertise and collaboration. Throughout the curriculum-mapping process, teachers engage in both reflecting on the taught curriculum and planning for the future. Both backward (journal) mapping and forward (projection) mapping invite teachers to create current, reality-based, and standards-aligned curricula.

Curriculum alignment. What does the ESL curriculum look like in your district? When we pose this question to teachers, the answers vary greatly.

We hear anything from "I don't have a set curriculum; I have kids from kindergarten to fifth grade often all at the same time in my class; I have to focus on the four language skills" to "I follow the state standards for ESL; I am a content-support ESL teacher, and my job is to pre-teach or re-teach what the students learn in their classes to be able to graduate from high school" to citing a commercially produced ESL program as the mandated curriculum.

Carefully conducted curriculum alignment is expected to result in the following:

1. ESL curriculum aligned to grade-level literacy/English language arts program

2. ESL curriculum aligned to grade-level content courses

3. ESL curriculum that integrates both grade-level literacy and content courses

If the ESL program does have a strong, purposeful connection to the grade-level content through curriculum alignment, instruction in the content classes becomes more meaningful for ELLs. Without such curriculum alignment, the ESL services may become fragmented, the content delivered in each class may become disjointed, and the skills introduced and practiced may become confusing and meaningless for ELLs.

What Research Says:

Over a decade ago, Collier and Thomas (2004) discussed the importance of keeping ELLs connected to the general education curriculum. Yet we still have more curriculum work to do to recognize and respond to the challenges ELLs face when trying to catch up to their English-speaking peers:

> If students are isolated from the curricular mainstream for many years, they are likely to lose ground to those in the instructional mainstream, who are constantly pushing ahead. To catch up to their peers, students below grade-level must make more than one year's progress every year to eventually close the gap. (p. 2)

Glatthorn, Boschee, and Whitehead (2006) argued that curriculum alignment was "a process of ensuring that the written, the taught, and the tested curricula are closely congruent" (p. 278). They cautioned that high-quality instruction requires clear, explicit learning goals. In too many schools, they observed a disconnect among key components of effective schooling—state standards, district curriculum guides or frameworks, the teachers' instructional plans, and their actual lesson delivery. They found that the assessment measures may be disjointed as well. It has also been suggested that aligning curriculum vertically and horizontally will be closely tied to professional development activities that allow teachers to examine their own practices and collaboratively improve instruction for their students.

Though neither Udelhofen (2005) nor Glatthorn et al. (2006) focus specifically on the purpose and outcome of curriculum mapping or alignment for the sake of ELLs, such curriculum development practices are expected to result in enhanced understanding of the general education curricula by ESL teachers and the ESL curriculum by general education teachers, thus resulting in a more deliberate, shared responsibility for ELLs.

A Leadership Voice From the Field

Josh L. Garfinkel, ELA/ESL Teacher Jefferson County Schools, Colorado:

As an English language arts/ESOL [English for speakers of other languages] professional in a high school that has a large number of language learners, one thing I have noticed is the importance of effective collaboration with teachers and administrators to enhance our students' acquisition of academic English. This is partly to ensure that opportunities for the type of rich communication (including reading and writing) that foster linguistic development occur continuously throughout the day and not just when the student is in English/ESL class. The only way to accelerate mastery of the curriculum for English learners is to work closely with the other stakeholders in our buildings, districts, and communities to facilitate maximum student understanding and proficiency in content area study while they are moving toward developing English proficiency. (personal communication, July 25, 2014)

PRACTICAL STEPS FOR COLLABORATIVE CURRICULUM IMPLEMENTATION

Elsewhere we discussed the five steps teams of teachers can take to incrementally move through standards-based curriculum implementation (Dove et al., 2014). Here, we revisit that structure to support an incremental, collaborative approach to translating curricula into successful classroom practice.

Step 1: As a team, become thoroughly familiar with both the mainstream and ELD standards and "unpack" them to understand the goals and expectations. Develop curricula aligned to these standards and reflect on whether the unit plans and lesson plans are appropriately supported and would help all students make reasonable progress toward the expectations.

Step 2: Initiate the standards-based curriculum implementation by encouraging teachers to try the aligned lessons and units, collect formative and summative assessment data, and keep careful notes as to what worked well for ELLs. Provider teachers should have frequent opportunities to engage in collaborative conversations in order to develop clarity about the expectations of the standards and ways of addressing the linguistic and sociocultural needs of the students.

Step 3: Help teachers become competent and confident when working with the newly created curricula so that they develop a sense of ownership of the curricula. Invite them to collaborate around the curricula, share resources and experiences, and exchange their growing repertoire of ideas about what the new curricula mean for ELLs. During this process, ensure there is a structure and clear expectations for outcomes. Nurture teacher leadership, and create opportunities for modeling and sharing successful practices.

Step 4: Collaboratively reflect on student data as evidence of progress and achievement. In this phase of implementation, curricular revisions and improvement will be the result of analyzing and reflecting on (a) formative and summative assessment, (b) student performance data, and (c) collaborative instructional practices.

Step 5: Invite teacher leaders to promote and advocate for the standards-based curricula to be implemented, with appropriate modifications or adaptations for diverse learners. Teachers should also partner with colleagues in professional development efforts.

Determining Shared Curriculum Responsibilities

Most recently, the changing role of the ESL teacher has become a frequently addressed topic by multiple professional organizations, researchers, and practitioners. Teachers and administrators alike agree on the need to redefine ESL/ELD teachers' positions in that they "should be recognized as experts, consultants, and trainers well versed in teaching rigorous academic content to ELLs" (Staehr Fenner, 2013b, p. 9). In fact, ESL/ELD teachers' expertise is critical in analyzing the academic language demands of the content curriculum, developing and modeling lessons that successfully address academic language and content simultaneously, scaffolding oral language and literacy development, and coaching general education teachers in the most effective, standards-based instruction for ELLs. Instead of feeling marginalized and isolated—as is often the case—ESL/ELD teachers need to be nurtured into leadership roles. How to best achieve that? Allow for frequent opportunities to showcase their unique knowledge and skill set, recognize and utilize them as indispensible resources within and outside the school community, and invite them to provide ongoing, job-embedded professional learning opportunities to their colleagues through simple conversations, more structured learning routines, and so on. By the same token, the entire school faculty needs to embrace their roles not just as K–5 general education teachers or 6–12 content specialists, but as teachers of academic language and disciplinary literacy (Dove et al., 2014; Gottlieb & Ernst-Slavin, 2014). See more on achieving this through professional development in Chapter 6 and through collaborative leadership in Chapter 7.

EXPANDING SHARED KNOWLEDGE AND COLLABORATIVE LEADERSHIP PRACTICES

The following resources and collaborative professional activities are designed to support your efforts as an administrator and instructional leader to build and expand a solid knowledge base about ESL/ELD programs and to develop a high-quality curriculum.

Key Resources

If you wish to review sound, locally developed ELD/ELL curriculum maps, visit the following school districts' websites:

- *Austin Independent School District, TX:*
  http://curriculum.austinisd.org/bil_ed/curriculum/ESOL1.html
- *Durham Public Schools, NC:* http://cia.dpsnc.net/esl/esl-ela-curriculum-links
- *Haverhill, Public Schools, MA:* http://www.haverhill-ps.org/curriculum-department/ell/
- *Holyoke Public Schools, MA:* http://www.hps.holyoke.ma.us/curriculummap.htm#ell
- *Oakland Schools, MI:* http://oaklandk12-public.rubiconatlas.org/Atlas/Browse/View/Curriculum

If you want to consider technology-enhanced curriculum mapping, try these:

- *Atlas Curriculum Mapping:* http://www.rubicon.com/Atlas CurriculumMapping.php
- *Curriculum Trak:* http://www.dynamic-internet-solutions.com/cur riculum-trak.cfm
- *BuildYourOwnCurriculum:* http://www.schoolsoftwaregroup.com/ BuildYourOwnCurriculum/CurriculumSoftware.aspx
- *Curriculum Mapper®:* http://www.clihome.com/solutions/curricu lum-mapper-features.aspx
- *TODCM:* http://todcm.org

If you want to check out curricular guidelines, frameworks, or ELD/ESL curriculum exemplars from state departments of education (DOE), visit these sites:

- *New Jersey DOE:* http://www.state.nj.us/education/bilingual/cur riculum/
- *New York DOE:* https://www.engageny.org/common-core-curricu lum
- *California DOE:* http://www.cde.ca.gov/ci/rl/cf/elaeldfrm-wrkchptrs2014.asp

Activities for Professional Learning

1. Examine the curriculum-planning template developed by Julie A. Motta and discussed in a recent blog post on www.colorincolorado .org. With your faculty, discuss the dimensions of the tool that are helpful in your own context and make adjustments to the tool as needed. (See https://ccweta.files.wordpress.com/2014/06/final-template-for-curriculum-work1.pdf)

2. Tung and her colleagues (2011) examined the intersection of curriculum, instruction, and assessment in select, high-performing, and significantly improving urban schools for English language learners. The following four themes emerged as consistent practice:

   o Designing and implementing a coherent, standards-based curriculum, sheltered for ELLs
   o Explicitly teaching all aspects of the English language and giving ample opportunities to use them
   o Utilizing ELLs' native language strategically to ensure that students understand tasks, vocabulary, and metacognitive strategies

o Using multiple forms of assessments that inform teachers' instruction

Consider what types challenges would have to be overcome to successfully implement each of these practices. Select the ones that are most aligned to your current practices and needs, and initiate a team approach to working on them.

3. Under the leadership of Kenji Hakuta, members of the Understanding Language Initiative at Stanford University (2013) identified six principles of standards-based instruction for ELLs:

   o Instruction focuses on providing ELLs with opportunities to engage in discipline-specific practices designed to build conceptual understanding and language competence in tandem.
   o Instruction leverages ELLs' home language(s), cultural assets, and prior knowledge.
   o Standards-aligned instruction for ELLs is rigorous, grade-level appropriate, and provides deliberate and appropriate scaffolds.
   o Instruction moves ELLs forward by taking into account their English proficiency level(s) and prior schooling experiences.
   o Instruction fosters ELLs' autonomy by equipping them with the strategies necessary to comprehend and use language in a variety of academic settings.
   o Diagnostic tools and formative assessment practices are employed to measure students' content knowledge, academic language competence, and participation in disciplinary practices. (p. 1)

Unpack each of these principles and discuss what they would look like in action to support curriculum development for ELLs in your school.

4 How Do You Support Collaborative Instructional and Assessment Practices for ELLs?

Do not confine your children to your own learning, for they were born in another time.

—Hebrew proverb

Richard J. Taibi, Principal, J. Harvey Rodgers School (former), Dorothy L. Bullock School, Glassboro, New Jersey, presents the outcomes of a pilot initiative:

The benefits of collaborative practice amongst educators are numerous and well documented, with one of the most important being collective ownership of student achievement. This ownership is of particular significance when working with our English language learners. As the majority of their instructional day is spent with teachers other than an ELL specialist, systemic routines must be established to ensure that the ELL specialist(s) and classroom teachers regularly review formative data and plan accordingly, using each other's expertise to design high-quality instruction. After all, we know that "it takes a village to raise a child!"

This collective ownership is a concept that has been successfully piloted at the J. Harvey Rodgers School (in Glassboro, NJ), and has resulted in significant social-emotional, oral-language, and literacy growth amongst our kindergarten ELLs. Our approach to achieving collective ownership has consisted of the following initiatives:

- *The inclusion of classroom teachers in professional learning routines that are typically only provided to the ELL staff. These routines encompass districtwide collaborative meetings/book studies and have helped us to ensure that the classroom teacher is applying research-based, best practices for our ELL students.*
- *Monthly one-on-one collaboration time between the ELL specialist & classroom teachers for planning and data review. A substitute teacher is provided for this formalized routine so that the two teachers can focus on developing content area or literacy instruction with the needs of our ELL students in mind. This planning time is in addition to any grade-level or team meetings or informal collaboration routines.*
- *The development of systemic "push-in" routines throughout our 60-minute guided reading block. During this time, the ELL specialist provides direct small-group instruction that includes guided reading, the development of schema, and vocabulary support. These practices are designed as both pre-teaching and follow-up support that is directly aligned to content area instruction. This activity is in addition to any instructional routines provided by the classroom teacher.*
- *Last (but not least) are ongoing collaboration, data review, and support in the form of walkthroughs with the building administration. This ongoing dialog has resulted in the establishment of best practices and has helped to ensure a learning environment where all teachers (and all students) are supported!* (personal communication, July 21, 2014)

How do we know what to teach English language learners (ELLs)? How can we make sure that our instruction is effective with them? How do we ascertain if they grow linguistically, academically, and socially as a result of our instruction that takes place in the classroom? The teaching-learning cycle becomes even more complex when students have to simultaneously master content and language, while they are also adjusting to a new culture and deciphering new norms and customs in their school and communities.

ESSENTIAL KNOWLEDGE

We have experienced a shift in English as a second language (ESL) or English language development (ELD) instructional and assessment practices in recent years (Rothenberg & Fisher, 2007). Developing academic language, general content area literacy skills, as well as disciplinary literacy skills are critical for students to successfully participate in academic work (Gottlieb & Ernst-Slavin, 2014; Zacarian, 2013; Zwiers, 2014). It is evident that all teachers (not just ESL and bilingual teachers) share the responsibility for engaging their students in academic language practices, and for building oral and written language skills closely tied to the content being taught. As Gottlieb and Ernst-Slavin remind us, teaching academic discourses is particularly important for "those students for whom English is a second, third, or fourth language and for students from underrepresented backgrounds who may not be surrounded by the types of thought and academic registers valued in schools" (p. 25).

There is also an increased emphasis on designing formative and summative assessments that accurately and reliably measure students' linguistic and academic growth. To ensure that instruction and assessment practices are congruent across your school building, collaboration in every phase of instruction—planning, delivery, assessment, and reflection—will be essential. As the World-Class Instructional Design and Assessment (WIDA) Consortium (2014) also recognized, "Given the diversity of students and teachers, no isolated theory or approach is adequate to guide the learning and teaching of all language learners" (p. 6). Here we briefly present seminal information on instructional and assessment practices for ELLs, with the understanding that the knowledge base in this field continuously expands; ongoing and emerging research challenges our thinking and guides our actions regarding ESL services.

The Collaborative Instructional Cycle

The professional literature documenting inclusive practices for students with disabilities as well as for ELLs has been expanding (Causton & Theoharis, 2014; Friend & Cook, 2012; Murawski, 2005; Villa, Thousand, & Nevin, 2013). Many researchers of inclusive education and practitioners in inclusive schools alike emphasize the need to engage in a complete cycle of collaboration. The collaborative instructional cycle—consisting of collaborative planning, instruction, assessment, and reflection (see Figure 4.1)—maximizes teacher effectiveness. Removing any of the four elements disrupts the balance and negatively impacts student learning. In addition to co-teaching or other collaborative instructional delivery, teachers need time and structured opportunities to (a) think deeply about differentiated unit and lesson planning, (b) gather and assess formative student data, and (c) reflect on the teaching-learning process that took place in the class (Schon, 1990).

Learning?

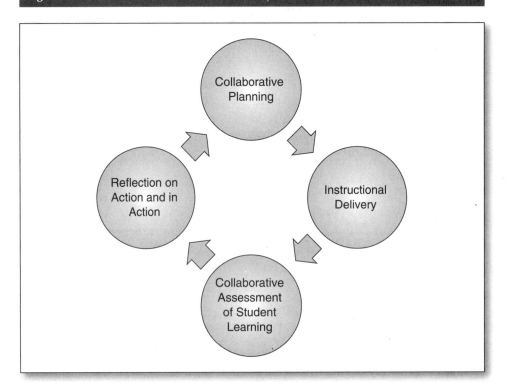

Figure 4.1 The Collaborative Instructional Cycle

Collaborative Planning

According to Chapman and Hyatt (2011), teachers need to take a problem-solving approach to preparing for co-teaching and engage in critical conversations around the following four dimensions of shared instructional practice:

1. Engaging with each other to establish the partnership and to lay the foundation for collaboration

2. Examining student data to make instructional decisions

3. Enhancing instruction to utilize both professionals' expertise

4. Expanding impact on student learning through systemic efforts for collaboration

The actual process of co-planning is most frequently understood as unit or lesson planning between two or more educators. Villa and Thousand (2005) observed, "Although many incentives appeal to specific individuals, the one incentive that is common to and highly valued by everyone engaged in education and educational reform is time—time for shared reflection and planning with colleagues" (p. 65). The most frequently cited challenge to collaboration is lack of time, so we urge you to make this your top priority: Consider all the creative ways you can provide time for teachers to work together for a sustained amount of time, on a regular basis, with clear goals and agendas in place (Howard & Potts, 2009; Murawski, 2005; Murawski & Dieker, 2008; Stetson, 2014).

Instructional Delivery Through Co-Teaching or Parallel Teaching

ESL/ELD services may be delivered as a stand-alone class period, during which ELLs go to a specially designated location and participate in small- or large-group instruction. When the ESL/ELD teacher provides services in a separate location, the greatest challenge to overcome at the elementary level is to consider what teaching and learning would be missed by the children removed from the general education classroom. And at the secondary level, the greatest challenge is to determine how ESL/ELD services can contribute to the necessary credits for graduation. If the ESL/ELD curriculum is aligned to grade-appropriate instruction and if pull-out services take place during English language arts (ELA) or other content area classes, the stand-alone program may be structured to address both the language development needs of ELLs and offer parallel instruction during the missed class period by focusing on the same learning targets, the same skills, or the same topic (through pre-teaching or re-teaching) as the rest of the class.

The ESL/ELD class period may also be a regularly built into ELLs' schedules, in which case they would not miss general education content instruction. When the ESL/ELD service delivery takes place within the context of a single classroom, both ESL/ELD and content teachers are equal instructional partners who combine their expertise and talents to make instruction rigorous, relevant, and carefully aligned to the general education expectations, while utilizing research-informed, evidence-based best practices (Honigsfeld & Dove, 2013).

Co-Teaching Models

In our work with ESL teachers and their general education colleagues, we have observed the following seven co-teaching arrangements. In the first three models, the teachers work with one large group of students. In the next three models, there are two groups of students split between the two cooperating teachers. In the final model, multiple groups of students are engaged in a learning activity that is facilitated and monitored by two teachers. Each of these configurations may have a place in any co-taught classroom, regardless of the grade level or the content area taught. As our research has progressed, we have also observed variations on these models that teaching teams have devised, which are also quite practical, beneficial, and supportive of co-teaching students.

Invite your teachers to discuss both the advantages and challenges of each and pilot various models in their classes to see which ones allow them to respond best to the students' needs, the specific content being taught, the type of learning activities designed, and the participating teachers' teaching styles and preferences. Encourage teachers to make strategic decisions about selecting one or more models for each lesson and help them articulate the reasons behind their choices as well as their desired student learning outcomes (see Table 4.1).

1. One group: one lead teacher and one teacher "teaching on purpose"

2. One group: two teachers teach same content

3. One group: one teaches, one assesses

4. Two groups: two teachers teach same content

5. Two groups: one teacher pre-teaches, one teacher teaches alternative information

6. Two groups: one teacher re-teaches, one teacher teaches alternative information

7. Multiple groups: two teachers monitor and teach

A more detailed discussion of each of these models is available in Chapters 4 and 5 of the companion book: *Collaboration and Co-Teaching: Strategies for English Learners* (Honigsfeld & Dove, 2010a). Keep in mind that no one model should be used exclusively: A combination of two to four models within a class period are feasible and advisable depending upon the content, strategies, and skills being addressed. Teachers may creatively develop their own variations on these models to further enhance their effectiveness.

Leadership Voices From the Field

Mary Beth Fortney, Principal at Marvin Elementary School, and Debra Cole, ELL Instructional Specialist for the St. Louis Region, Missouri, discuss the importance of employing differentiated instructional strategies in a collaborative teaching context:

It is much more effective having the ELL teacher working as a co-teacher for the whole class, rather than as a push-in teacher to assist only the ELLs. This is because all students benefit from the ELL strategies and differentiated instruction and from the strong relationships both teachers have with all of the students. Our biggest challenge with the co-teaching model occurs when the ELL teacher leaves the classroom. We plan to address this challenge by providing monthly professional development for classroom teachers to be better able to differentiate for their ELLs. This professional development will be open to all teaching staff but focused on the classroom teachers with an ELL cluster group—where ELLs are integrated with grade-level peers for their content instruction. (personal communication, July 24, 2014)

Table 4.1 Seven Co-Teaching Models

Co-Teaching Model	Description	Class Setup
One student group: One lead teacher and another teacher teaching on purpose	The mainstream and ESL teachers take turns assuming the lead role. One leads while the other provides minilessons to individuals or small groups in order to pre-teach or clarify a concept or skill.	
One student group: Two teachers teach the same content	Both teachers direct a whole-class lesson and work cooperatively to teach the same lesson at the same time.	
One student group: One teacher teaches, one assesses	Two teachers are engaged in conducting the same lesson; one teacher takes the lead, and the other circulates throughout the room and assesses targeted students through observations, checklists, and anecdotal records.	

(Continued)

Table 4.1 (Continued)

Co-Teaching Model	Description	Class Setup
Two student groups: Two teachers teach the same content	Students are divided into two learning groups. The teachers engage in parallel teaching, presenting the same content using differentiated learning strategies.	A,B,C = A,B,C
Two student groups: One teacher pre-teaches, one teaches alternative information	Teachers assign students to one of two groups based on their readiness levels related to a designated topic or skill. Students who have limited prior knowledge of the target content or skill are grouped together to receive instruction to bridge the gap in their background knowledge.	A,B,C ≠ D,E,F
Two student groups: One teacher re-teaches, one teaches alternative information	Flexible grouping provides students at various proficiency levels with the support they need for specific content. Student group composition changes as needed.	A,B,C / A,B,C ≠ D,E,F
Multiple student groups: Two teachers monitor and teach	Multiple groupings allow both teachers to monitor and facilitate student work while targeting selected students with assistance for their particular learning needs.	

ELD INSTRUCTIONAL PRACTICES

Whether co-taught or parallel taught, high-quality instructional practices will be critical to student success. One such practice, the focus on academic language, which first appeared with the Cognitive Academic Language Learning Approach or CALLA (Chamot & O'Malley, 1987, 1994), has been integrated with content instruction and explicit learning strategy instruction. Since CALLA, various interpretations of *sheltering* have been developed to enable ELLs to study grade-appropriate content—the same content their monolingual English counterparts are learning.

The SIOP Model

A common characteristic of all sheltered classes is that ELLs receive special assistance to help them understand general education course content while also developing a broad range of language skills. Echevarria, Vogt, and Short (2008, 2012), along with a large team of ESL/ELD and general education practitioners, developed a comprehensive model known today as the *Sheltered Instruction Observation Protocol*, or SIOP. The SIOP Model consists of eight major components (preparation, building background, comprehensible input, strategies, interaction, practice/application, lesson delivery, and review/evaluation) and thirty subcomponents or instructional strategies centering on the concept that each lesson teachers deliver must be built on matching language and content objectives to allow ELLs to acquire both necessary linguistic skills and academic-content knowledge.

The features that most set SIOP apart from high-quality instruction for native English speakers include (a) extended wait time, (b) teaching key vocabulary, (c) adapting content to ELLs' background knowledge and language proficiency levels, (d) language objectives, (e) clarification in the students' native language, (f) modifying one's speech to be appropriate for ELLs' proficiency levels, (g) using a range of supplementary materials, and (h) explicitly connecting new learning to students' background experiences. SIOP is among the most widely utilized instructional frameworks in U.S. schools with over 400 schools/districts working on large scale implementation (Jana Echevarria, personal communication, August 19, 2014).

ExC-ELL

Calderón (2007) conducted extensive research on effective content-based literacy instructional practices for adolescent ELLs and designed a framework of instruction named Expediting Comprehension for English Language Learners (ExC-ELL). ExC-ELL is a lesson planning and delivery system focusing on accelerating content and language attainment through the systematic implementation of the following ten key components:

1. Content standards, objectives, indicators, purpose, outcomes, and targets
2. Parsing of text by teachers
3. Summarization or overview of unit, lesson, or chapter
4. Background building of concepts
5. Review previous lesson, concepts, or content
6. Systematic vocabulary instruction
7. Formulate questions for drawing background knowledge
8. Engagement with text
9. Consolidation of content and skills
10. Assessments (pp. 14–15)

ExC-ELL has been documented to result in increased achievement when the whole school is implementing the academic language, reading comprehension, and writing instructional strategies. It has been successfully implemented in numerous parts of the United States, including New York City (MS 319), Charlotte-Mecklenburg, North Carolina (Winterfield Elementary), and Salt Lake City (Granite Park MS), where students attained substantial growth in one year, advancing from average- or low-performing to high-performing schools. All students, ELLs in particular, benefited. These schools were designated demonstration schools by each district, inviting other schools to visit and learn from them. Middle and high schools in five districts in the State of Virginia have also been designated ExC-ELL for Science schools, where specific data will be gathered to further the connection between ExC-ELL and STEM (science, technology, engineering, and mathematics) (M. Calderon, July 15, 2014, personal communication).

Quality Teaching for English Learners (QTEL)

Under the leadership of Aida Walqui, the WestEd professional team developed QTEL in response to the challenges of preparing ELLs to be college and career ready. The six principles that undergird this professional learning framework are designed to prepare teachers of ELLs to challenge their learners while also offering high levels of support to them in all areas of language and content development (http://qtel.wested.org). These principles are as follows:

- Maintain academic rigor
- Set high expectations
- Focus on metaprocesses (student awareness of the processes, strategies, and outcomes of their own learning)
- Create opportunities and sustain quality interactions with peers and teachers
- Focus on language learning in disciplinary contexts
- Develop a quality curriculum with a spiraling progression and ample scaffolding

QTEL has been a highly regarded, successfully implemented framework of professional development and ESL/ELD instruction in school districts around the country, including those in New York, California, and Texas.

SHARED KNOWLEDGE BASE OF VARIOUS MODELS OF INSTRUCTION

What is common in all these approaches is the intentional integration of content and language instruction, making sure learning is strategically planned, structured, scaffolded, and comprehensible. In her call for an Academic Language Campaign, Kinsella (2012) urged educators working with increasingly diverse student populations to "simultaneously teach rigorous content while modeling and coaching adept academic English register with integrity and tenacity" (p. 23). The greatest emphasis might be on connecting content and language in every class, yet equally important is ensuring that an assets-based model of instruction (Walqui & van Lier, 2010) is enacted, in which educators (a) value and validate students' native language and home cultures, (b) make connections to students' lives and systematically build the necessary background knowledge, and (c) bridge prior skills and new ones for students to participate in the learning process. To accomplish all this requires K–12 general education teachers to become thoroughly familiar with second-language acquisition, sociocultural processes of learning, and the features of academic English and disciplinary literacy. At the same time, these teachers need to grow comfortable with infusing language practice in their instruction, holding ELLs to high but reasonable expectations, and maintaining academic rigor in their content classes. On the other hand, ESL/ELD teachers will need to be able to offer content-based and content-supported language-learning opportunities that advance ELLs' educational progress as well as foster their social and academic language.

COLLABORATIVE ASSESSMENT: INTRODUCING CULTURALLY AND LINGUISTICALLY RESPONSIVE PRACTICES

O'Malley and Valdez Pierce (1996) noted six purposes for assessing ELLs: (1) screening to identify ELLs, (2) placing ELLs in appropriate language support programs, (3) reclassifying ELLs or exiting them from language support programs, (4) monitoring ELLs' progress, (5) evaluating ESL/ELD programs, and (6) providing data for accountability measures. Staehr Fenner (2013a) and Hauck, Wolf, and Mislevy (2013) identified several overarching reasons why equitable assessment practices—ones that are valid, reliable, and fair—are essential for accurately gauging English-language development and academic achievement:

1. Correct identification, classification, placement, and reclassification of ELLs based on their language proficiency levels. Valid and reliable assessment measures will ensure this.

2. Effective instruction. If both general education and ESL/ELD teachers have meaningful, accurate, and actionable assessment data about their ELLs' language development and content attainment, they can plan more effective lessons, differentiate instruction more purposefully, and integrate content learning with language development opportunities across the four domains of listening, speaking, reading, and writing.

3. Transparent accountability. Since data on ELLs are integral to school, district, and state accountability systems, they must accurately document ELLs' development both in language proficiency and academic attainment.

Fisher and Frey (2007) make a compelling case for checking for understanding and conducting formative assessments that inform instruction. Among others, Gottlieb (2006), Guskey and Jung (2013), Jung and Guskey (2012), and Staehr Fenner (2013a) recommend a multiple-measure assessment system to be established that includes formative and summative assessment measures. These assessment practices will need to address both content and language development, with the types of accommodations that are most conducive to the students' language proficiency level.

School leaders need to establish a collaboratively developed, fair, and equitable class and school grading and reporting policy that has a clear purpose, aligned to standards, supported by research (Guskey, 2014). To ensure that all stakeholders can celebrate successes without losing touch of what is expected of students at a particular grade level or content area, make sure you include measures to report both student growth in language development and academic attainment as well as core content achievement in relation to grade-level standards and/or benchmarks. "Focusing solely on growth will lead stakeholders to believe that our ELLs are on target; however, they may still be a long way off from where they need to be. Focusing solely on benchmarks will devalue all that our students (and teachers) have accomplished" (R. J. Taibi, personal communication, July 27, 2014).

Reflection

As Schön (1990) stated, reflective practitioners engage both in *reflection in action* (while being engaged in a classroom experience with students) and *reflection on action* (through action research and lifelong learning). Airasian and Gullickson (1994) suggested that teachers develop scientific or technical knowledge in their teacher preparation programs, but experiential learning takes place once they are practicing in the classroom and are *learning by doing*. They claim that "it is the constant cycle of experience, reflection, and improvement that marks a teacher's growth and development; teachers do learn by doing, but only if they also reflect upon, critique, and base future actions on knowledge gained from past actions" (p. 195). We adapted Osterman and Kottkamp's (2004) outline of reflective practice developed for professional development and applied it to collaborative instructional practices. Figure 4.2 represents the purpose and context of collaborative reflective practices, assumptions underlying such practices, and strategies used to engage in reflections.

TRANSFER TO PRACTICE

Building Teacher Teams Through Collaborative Planning

Finding the time for co-planning is one of the most frequently discussed challenges teachers face. Since co-planning is the corner stone of creating strong teacher teams, make it a priority to schedule adequate time for teachers who discuss student needs, standards and grade-level curricular expectations, successful instructional practices that are connected assessment data, and specifics of lessons. Co-planning allows for consistency of instructional and assessment strategies to be implemented across grades and subject matters as well as for job-embedded, ongoing professional learning. Through sharing their expertise and experiences, through honest conversations about what works and what does not, and through

Figure 4.2 Reflective Practice for Collaborative Endeavors

Reflective Practice

Purpose	To understand our own teaching and our colleagues' teaching To build on our own shared competencies

Assumptions	Learning is co-constructed. Learning is personally and interpersonally meaningful. Knowledge is a shared tool.

Context	Job-embedded learning Experiential, classroom-based knowledge construction

Strategies	Reflective journals or logs Collaborative conversations Collaborative inquiry Peer coaching and mentoring Collaborative action research

SOURCE: Honigsfeld and Dove (2010 a, p. 153).

focused attention to lesson planning with ELLs in mind, teachers regularly engage in professional exchanges that significantly contributes to their own learning—ultimately benefitting all students.

Figure 4.3 A Standard-Based Co-Planning Template

Date:	Class:	Collaborative Teachers:

Standards Addressed

Learning Objectives (Content/Language)

Activities/Tasks (Rigor and Engagement)

Co-Teachers' Roles/Co-Teaching Models

Resources and Materials

Technology Integration

Accommodations/Modifications

Formative and/or Summative Assessment Procedure

Reflections/Special Notes

SOURCE: Adapted from Honigsfeld and Dove (2013).

Encourage your teachers to adapt this template and insert additional lesson-planning headings as needed. To ensure the co-planning sessions are most productive, we suggest that teachers establish an easy-to-maintain routine or protocol. A co-planning agenda with clear, easy-to-implement, manageable steps is likely to yield the desired results. The *Sample Standards-Based Co-Planning Agenda* in Figure 4.1 may also be expanded and modified as needed.

Box 4.1   Sample Standards-Based Co-Planning Agenda

1. Review previous unit or lesson and student assessment data

2. Select target standards

3. Determine unit or lesson goals, objectives, or learning targets

4. Identify instructional procedures

5. Differentiate instructional and assessment strategies

6. Assign roles and responsibilities for individual follow-up planning

---

Co-planning time may also be used effectively for co-developing instructional materials that are tiered and reflective of multiple-language proficiency or readiness levels that exist in any class. This shared activity promotes exploring differentiated learning; it supports collaborating teachers in their efforts to decide on how to accelerate the curriculum, how to select essential learning targets, and how to scaffold the challenging aspects of the content. Once co-planning is successfully established, allow for teacher leadership to emerge, and nurture it by inviting teacher teams to present both the process and the product (outcomes) of their collaborative efforts. Making teacher teams' successes and challenges transparent to the larger school community empowers and inspires others and leads to continuous improvement.

Supporting Collaborative Teaching

Being in a leadership position, your role is critical to make sure teachers are invited or carefully selected and paired up to form co-teaching teams. They also need training, time to build trust, and opportunities for professional relationships. Ongoing coaching and intervisitations allow teachers to observe each other in a nonjudgmental, nonevaluative manner. Though these are informal observations, establishing a protocol or using an observation tool is very beneficial (Saide & Fox, 2014). Co-teaching teams need feedback and support regarding their co-teaching practices. We designed an observation and coaching tool named I-TELL (Integrated Teaching for ELLs Observation Tool) to aid administrators, instructional leaders, coaches, and peer visitors in identifying features of successful co-teaching practices for the sake of ELLs. The tool in Figure 4.4 allows for direct collection of evidence on each of the collaborative indicators.

When observing co-teachers in action—co-delivering instruction—some additional look-fors include the following:

- **Parity:** Do both teachers participate equitably in the lesson (not equally)?
- **Integration of language skills:** Do both teachers provide instruction and support for content and language development?
- **Opportunities to talk:** Does the smaller student-teacher ratio lead to higher levels of student-to-student interaction and more student talk for academic purposes?
- **Engagement**: Do both teachers provide students with meaningful, challenging learning activities that make engagement visible?
- **Formative assessment use**: Do the co-teachers collect and respond to formative assessment data to offer immediate intervention as needed, and as a result maximize the benefits of co-teaching?

Leadership Voice From the Field

Shaeley Santiago, Instructional Coach, Ames Community School District, Iowa, makes a case for systemic support for collaboration:

Quality collaboration is created at the systemic level. It requires a culture of respect of others, shared responsibility for the success of all learners, and the structures (such as common planning time) for collaboration to happen. Co-teaching is one such structure. Teachers who co-teach learn from each other and can play off each other's strengths. Their combined efforts can provide a great benefit to students who receive targeted language instruction while accessing the core. (personal communication, July 25, 2014)

Protocol for Co-Assessment

Collaborative planning time must include an analysis and response to student data. In addition to discussing assessment measures and assessment tools, the co-assessment planning sessions will also need to focus on

Figure 4.4 I-TELL Observation Tool

	No Evidence	Emerging Evidence	Adequate Evidence	Exceptional Evidence	Documentation/ Comments
Co-teachers collaboratively plan and develop instructional materials for the lesson					
Equity between the co-teachers is established from the onset of the lesson and maintained throughout the lesson					
Language and content objectives are addressed by both teachers					
Teaching roles and responsibilities are shared					
Two or more co-teaching models are used: Students in one group, teachers work together: • One leads, one teaches one purpose • Two teach same content • One teaches, one assesses Students in two groups, teachers work separately: • Two teach same content • One preteaches, one teaches alternative • One reteaches, one teaches alternative Students in multiple groups • Teachers monitor, facilitate and teach					

	No Evidence	Emerging Evidence	Adequate Evidence	Exceptional Evidence	Documentation/ Comments
Students are grouped purposefully in meaningful ways throughout the lesson					
Co-teachers interact with students and each other in ways that enhance student learning					
Co-teachers are familiar with and respond to the learning needs of all the students					
Co-teachers implement appropriate differentiated strategies for teaching academic language and content					
Co-teachers demonstrate respect and collegiality for each other throughout the lesson					
Co-teachers apply appropriate visual, graphic, linguistic and interpersonal scaffolds					
Co-teachers establish high levels of engagement and ensure all four language skills to be integrated: listening, speaking, reading, and writing					
Co-teachers collaboratively conduct formative and summative assessments					

what types of accommodations or modifications should be used to make sure fair and equitable assessment and grading practices are implemented (Jung & Guskey, 2012).

Once the assessment data have been collected, make sure teachers engage in carefully examining representative work by ELLs. In *Collaborative Analysis of Student Work: Improving Teaching and Learning,* Langer, Colton, and Gott (2003) suggested the use of rubrics and protocols within a framework of collaborative conversations and inquiry. We, too, encourage the use of a protocol that helps teachers examine student work by focusing on four unique dimensions. For an in-depth, structured discussion of student work, introduce the *Sampling Work by English Language Learners* (SWELL) protocol and encourage teachers to share the challenges ELLs and they face. See Box 4.2 for the guiding questions, grouped in four categories.

Box 4.2 Protocol for Sampling Work by English Language Learners

Invite teachers to collaboratively examine literacy and content-based work samples by ELLs and consider the following questions, organized in four subcategories for their joint exploration of student learning:

1. Academic language/linguistic development

   a. What stage of second-language acquisition is evident?

   b. Which academic-language features has the student mastered and been able to use systematically?

   c. What are two or three prominent linguistic challenges the student's work demonstrates?

   d. Other comments

2. Disciplinary or content-based academic needs

   a. What are two or three examples of successfully acquired ELA or content-specific knowledge and/or skills?

   b. What are some noticeable gaps in the student's prior knowledge?

   c. What are some gaps in the student's new skills and discipline-specific knowledge attainment?

   d. What ELA domain-specific subskills (listening, speaking, reading, writing) does the student need to work on?

   e. Other comments

3. Cultural experiences and challenges

    a. In what way are the student's cultural experiences reflected in his or her work?

    b. Is there any evidence that the student was struggling with cultural misunderstandings or misconceptions?

    c. Other comments

4. Social-emotional aspects of learning

    a. Is there evidence of motivated, self-directed learning in the student's work sample?

    b. Has the learner been engaged in the task?

    c. Is there evidence of task persistence?

    d. Is there evidence of being engaged in cooperative learning (peer editing, etc.)?

    e. Other comments

SOURCE: Adapted from Honigsfeld and Dove (2013).

Creating and Supporting Teacher Inquiry Communities

For reflection to happen and become internalized, teachers need the opportunity to engage in it. Some of us are by nature more reflective; driving home from school, we replay the events that took place, the interactions we had with others, and the choices we made during the day. However, for reflection to be transferred into a collaborative context, teachers need the space and time to do it—"moving out from the isolation of the classroom to the shelter of inquiry communities that provided safe spaces for real dialogue, the sharing of stories, relationships with colleagues" (Waff, 2009, pp. 70–71).

Among so many others, Goodlad, Mantle-Bromley, and Goodlad (2004) recommended teachers engage in a process of inquiry that consists of four cyclical, ongoing steps—dialogue, decision making, action, and evaluation—focused on a shared purpose. They claimed that such collaborative inquiry is "the single-most important vehicle for school renewal" (p. 110). For formative assessment purposes, similar to Gajda and Koliba (2008), we suggest adapting Goodlad et al.'s following four-step framework to your local context:

1. **Dialogue**: Regularly engage in preplanned professional dialogues about key instructional issues and ELLs' academic and linguistic development and performance.

2. **Decision making**: Collectively decide what collaborative practices you wish to initiate, develop, continue, or discontinue.

3. **Action**: Based on the collaborative decisions, actively engage in initiating, developing, continuing, or discontinuing certain practices.

4. **Evaluation**: Regularly collect and analyze both informal and formal data about both your teaching practices and ELL students' learning.

USING A REFLECTIVE FRAMEWORK FOR SCHOOL IMPROVEMENT

York-Barr, Sommers, Ghere, and Montie (2006) identified four levels of reflective practice to improve schools. When transferred into the collaborative ESL context, the four levels serve as critical guides for improving interpersonal and communication skills, as well as productivity. The contents of Table 4.2 are organized around the four overarching questions for reflection: What happened? Why? So what? Now what?

EXPANDING SHARED KNOWLEDGE AND COLLABORATIVE LEADERSHIP PRACTICES

The following resources and collaborative professional activities are designed to support your efforts as an administrator and instructional leader to build and expand a solid knowledge base about ESL/ELD programs and to develop a collaborative instructional cycle.

Key Resources

If you plan to explore research-based best practices for ELL instruction, visit the following sites:

- Center for Applied Linguistics: www.cal.org
- ExC-ELL: http://calderon.learningsciences.com
- GLAD (Guided Language Acquisition Design): http://www.project glad.com

Table 4.2   Four Critical Steps for Reflective Questions

1. What happened? (description)	2. Why? (analysis, interpretation)
• What did I do? What did others (e.g., co-teachers, students, adults) do? • What was my effect at the time? What was their effect? • What was going on around us? Where were we? When during the day did it occur? Was there anything unusual happening?	• Why do I think things happened in this way? • How might the context have influenced the experience? • Are there other potential contributing factors? • What are my hunches about why things happened the way they did?
3. So what? (overall meaning and application) • Why did this seem like a significant event to reflect on? • What have I learned from this? How could I improve? • How might this change my future thinking, behavior, or interactions? • What questions remain?	4. Now what? (implications for action) • Who should be actively included in reflecting on this event? • The next time a situation like this presents itself, how do I want to behave? • How can I set up conditions to increase the likelihood of productive interactions and learning?

SOURCE: Adapted from York-Barr, Sommers, Ghere, and Montie (2006).

- QTEL: http://qtel.wested.org/principles-of-quality-teaching-for-english-learners/
- SIOP: http://www.cal.org/siop/
- Understanding Language: http://ell.stanford.edu
- WIDA: www.wida.us
- Adolescent Literacy: http://www.adlit.org

If you wish to learn more about co-teaching both for ELLs and students with disabilities, visit the following sites:

- www.powerof2.com
- www.coteachingforells.weebly.com

If you are committed to building a professional library for all teachers to share, in collaboration with your faculty, carefully select books and subscribe to journals that keep the entire school faculty up-to-date on best practices for ELLs. See www.colorincolorado.org for recommended resources.

Activities for Professional Learning

1. Festus Oblakor and Christopher Yawn (2013) noted,

   The provision of quality curriculum and instruction is intertwined with culture, and that cultural relevance must be present
   in all aspects of teaching and learning to help bridge barriers
   between CLD [culturally and linguistically diverse] students
   and teachers, and families and schools. (p. 164)

Discuss the implications of this statement to the type of collaborative
curriculum work and the entire instructional cycle that is taking place in
your school. Explore opportunities to enhance the cultural relevance of the
planned, intended, and taught curricula.

2. Eleni Pappamihiel (2012) conducted several visits to a school and,
   based on her study of the challenges and success of implementing
   co-teaching, she concluded:

   Co-teaching is not putting two teachers together and asking them
   to work together with no common preparation time. Co-teaching
   is not using an ESL teacher as a floater for only the ESL students.
   Co-teaching is not one teacher entering another teacher's classroom without the power to influence instruction. Co-teaching is
   not the act of taking a qualified teacher and re-forming him/her
   into a teacher's aide. Finally, co-teaching does not replace other
   ESL services for students who are beginners and need more individualized instruction in addition to help in their mainstream
   classes. (p. 4)

As a team, discuss the points made in this excerpt. Create your own
lists of what co-teaching is and what it is not, and see if your faculty's
conclusions are similar to Pappamihiel's. Develop strategies to improve
the co-teaching arrangements in your school and agree on actionable steps
are needed to make sure co-teaching fulfills its promise and is implemented for the maximum benefit of students.

3. Discuss with your fellow instructional leaders to what extent you
   agree with the quote toward the beginning of the chapter by Villa
   and Thousand (2005): "Although many incentives appeal to specific
   individuals, the one incentive that is common to and highly valued
   by everyone engaged in education and educational reform is time—
   time for shared reflection and planning with colleagues" (p. 65).

What are your experiences related to this quote? What incentives does your school offer? How can the challenge of having enough time be effectively addressed within the constraints of the typical school day as well as outside of it?

4. Pilot the I-TELL tool presented in this chapter. Invite the collaborating teachers to add dimensions to this observation tool as needed and/or refine the criteria identified in the right-hand-side column of the chart.

5 What Are the Nuts and Bolts of Coordinating Collaborative Teaching for ELLs?

If a race could be won after the first gallop, thousands would wear blue ribbons.

—American folk saying

Jennifer Bradshaw, Assistant Superintendent for Instruction, Smithtown Central School District, New York, explains the tools and structures that are in place to support teacher collaboration:

Collaboration is critical to our students' success. Teachers deserve structures and administrative support to make collaboration not just possible but as effective as possible. Time, opportunities, training, expectations, and moral support are all necessary. Without collaboration—without a team of content specialists and expert differentiation for our English language learners and without a shared awareness of the unique abilities and culture of each student—we cannot maximize the impact of the precious hours we have with our students each day.

> *Our program is a work in progress, impeded by classic obstacles like inadequate staffing, funding, and shared planning time. Important improvements we made relied on collaboration among building and department administrators. When building leaders made English language learners a priority—by sharing department meeting time with the ESL department, by devoting technological and spatial resources, by celebrating the diversity of all learners—content area teachers were and are encouraged to engage more proactively in collaboration with their ESL colleagues. All levels of administration were trained and provided with the language to promote the social, emotional, and academic success of English language learners—that needs to be ongoing. ESL teachers were scheduled to meet with content area teachers to discuss differentiation and cultural awareness—that could happen more frequently. Weekly communication logs were established to increase the sharing of content area support needs with our ESL extra-help providers, and that has been very effective. To a large extent, we still rely on the passionate outreach of our dedicated ESL teachers to make collaboration happen. But we're improving, and many of these basic structures—communication logs, shared department time, and administrative training—take effort but not a whole lot of money.* (personal communication, July 21, 2014)

School leaders make various decisions on a daily basis; some of these decisions need to be made quickly without consultation while others need input from various members of the school community in order to reach the best possible outcomes. Navigating who should be involved in which type of decision can be the cause of some anxiety for administrators (Nye & Capelluti, 2003). Yet faculty and staff often rely on their leaders not to hesitate to take needed action or to have the appropriate answers. Nonetheless, when it comes to making decisions concerning school policies and programs for linguistically diverse populations of students, some leaders may not be as well versed or as confident to make those decisions on their own.

ESSENTIAL KNOWLEDGE

What can become problematic is a one-size-fits-all approach to decision making, and although following some standard framework for everyday procedures and routines is certainly invaluable, it can sometimes get in the way. For a case in point, let's consider an assistant principal who must decide on a class placement for a new student who has arrived after the academic year has begun. Now the classes have already been painstakingly balanced and set by grade-level teacher teams and reviewed by school specialists (e.g., English as a second language, or ESL, and special education teachers), guidance counselors, and building administrators. The number of students in each class has also been determined to be fairly even. After the school year has begun, the standard procedure is for the assistant principal to look at the number of students held by each class and place the student solely on that criterion.

The student to be placed, however, just arrived from China a little over a week ago with his family. He spoke absolutely no English whatsoever. Yet he was being assigned to a class due solely to class size—neither the teacher nor his classmates spoke any Chinese. In this scenario, the assistant principal was focused on setting an equal number of students per teacher, and in this day and age, with high-stakes testing and teacher evaluation tied to student assessment, it would seem to be a pretty fair decision. Yet in the class next door was a student fluent in both English and the new student's dialect of Chinese who could have lent him support. Shortly thereafter, a teacher who was concerned about this placement met with the assistant principal, and due to the shared decision-making relationship this leader had with her faculty, the child's placement was changed.

Out-of-the-Box Thinking

We strongly advocate for collaborative school practices that lead to what is often called *out-of-the-box* thinking and decision making. These notions work together with leadership support to rethink standard school practices for the sake of English language learners (ELLs). There are hidden inequities that occur through the development of regular policies and programs for all students, and they may contribute to a lack of desired educational outcomes for special student populations. For example, some schools segregate groups of students from regular class instruction for language learning, remediation, basic-skills development, and so on. Frattura and Capper (2007) described this practice as follows:

> Under a segregated program model, educators believe that the primary reason for student failure is the student him- or herself, that students cannot be helped until they fail and receive a label of some sort (at-risk, disability, low reader), and then the student is placed into a separate program that is removed from the core teaching and learning of the school or tracked into lower ability classes. (p. 13)

School leaders need to go beyond the usual frameworks and procedures to create equitable learning environments with linguistically diverse students in mind. Yet what might be equitable does not always size up to being equal. So what do school leaders need to know about creating organizational structures that support equitable teaching and learning for English learners? To begin, teacher collaboration and co-teaching can be the impetus for developing an effective framework for integrated teaching practices to accommodate the learning needs of English learners. How that framework will take shape—when and where it will all take place—will depend on each school, including the size of its ELL population, the number of ESL teachers available, the regulations state and local districts may have concerning collaborative teaching, and so on. These variables are some of the reasons why we say that out-of-the-box thinking is essential.

Teacher collaboration for the instruction of English learners includes various configurations of schoolwide teaching teams that share their knowledge, experience, time, expertise, and even physical classroom space to empower ELLs to grow linguistically, academically, socially, and emotionally (Honigsfeld & Dove, 2010a). In essence, "Each teacher brings to the planning table a wealth of knowledge about appropriate resources to meet individual student needs" (p. 150). These collaborative teams often spark out-of-the-box thinking, creatively meeting the challenges of working with this student population, most often with limited resources.

Promoting a Collaborative School Culture

We are certain from our observations and practical experience in the field that successful collaborative school teams do not magically happen. They develop from the makings of a strong school culture that supports the education of English learners. This population of students is often marginalized, and teachers frequently subscribe to a deficit model of thinking about ELLs—"holding lower expectations for students with demographics that do not fit the traditional context of the school system . . . [which] further alienates them from the contemporary school setting by perpetuating deficit attitudes and practices toward students who are marginalized" (Simone, 2012, para. 1). Consequently, school leaders must foster a school culture that invites honest teacher-to-teacher and teacher-to-leader talk to help eliminate deficit thinking and build truly inclusive policies, programs, and classroom practices for the sake of ELLs.

A Leadership Voice From the Field

Christopher Miller, EdD, Secondary Supervisor of Guidance, Harrison Central School District, New York, emphasizes the role pupil personnel departments play:

School counselors play a critical role in ensuring students and families are welcomed into the school system. From the moment of entrance, school counselors help students and their families to understand the school, transition into the environment and culture, and access needed services. Interpreting academic records from previous school settings is necessary to appropriately place and guide students in the new setting. Often, translation services are required to not only set a tone of support, but to more fully understand the students. The partnership with teachers of ELLs is integral to further facilitating a smooth transition. Teachers of ELLs are experts in helping to provide students what they need when they need it and this includes daily support through monitoring student progress and application of timely interventions. School counselors collaborate and can act in concert with teachers of ELLs to serve as liaisons between home and school and to support students in their new environment. Regular "check-ins" between school counselors and teachers of ELLs sustain the support required for these transitioning students. The transition to a new school for any student is challenging; for ELLs, the transition is compounded by the need to learn language and culture. The more support and attention that can be provided to ELLs and their families, the better we can ensure student needs are met. (personal communication, July 28, 2014)

Building Collaborative Teams

First and foremost, collaborative teams are the mainstay for any integrated service delivery model for the instruction of ELLs. Yet despite much evidence that collaboration works, time and again we hear how teacher collaboration does not just happen on its own. Piercey (2010) suggested if administrators wanted more teachers to collaborate, they would need to model the collaboration they so much want to see. He further identified one reason for the lack of teacher collaboration, which is that teachers are simply confused about what they are to do. Therefore, in order to form ideal collaborative teams, building capacity is key. Teachers need to know what is expected of them from collaborative teamwork, what role they will play among their team members, and what possible outcomes are expected.

In order to create collaborative team partnerships, we recommend the following strategies (Honigsfeld & Dove, 2010a):

- Develop shared goals for collaborative work.
- Establish regular opportunities for honest communication both between administrators and faculty as well as among teacher teams.
- Identify roles and individual responsibilities among team members.
- Explore the concepts of shared decision making in teams and how to reach consensus.
- Outline strategies to determine which decisions might be made individually and which should be made in consultation with team members.

Team membership can also be fluid, for example, consisting of a core team such as grade-level/content teachers and ESL specialists and inviting literacy, special education, music, and art faculty, as well as guidance counselors, social workers, and so on, to complement efforts to collaborate. In addition, paraprofessionals such as bilingual teacher assistants and classroom aides might enhance team planning with individual ELLs in mind. Administrators may also want to join in on team meetings from time to time.

The Value of Teacher Autonomy

For more than a decade, increasing numbers of educational decisions have been made on the federal and state levels of government. Beginning with the authorization of No Child Left Behind (2001), which brought about annual high-stakes testing for all students, and continuing with the Race to the Top initiative (2012), which promoted college- and career-ready standards as well as teacher evaluation, it might seem that much of what is done in the classroom has been taken out of the teachers' hands. Coupled with these enactments, some school districts have responded to meeting the demands of higher expectations by purchasing prepackaged programs to enhance instruction to meet higher standards. Although well-meaning administrators have instituted many of these programs, it only adds to the overwhelming amount of decisions that have been taken out of teachers' hands.

Combine all these changes with a movement toward teacher collaboration and teachers might truly feel they no longer have any autonomy to make instructional decisions. According to DuFour (2011),

> Some critics of systematic collaboration even offer a conspiracy theory, arguing that any effort to embed collaborative processes into the school day represents an administrative ploy to compel teachers to do the bidding of others and demonstrates a lack of commitment to empowering teachers. (p. 58)

The fact of the matter is that true teacher collaboration can be structured to empower teachers to make positive instructional change that reaches beyond individual classrooms. As a group, teachers can use their collective purpose and goals to make decisions about instructional content, skills, strategies, resources, materials, and assessments to create a truly cohesive program for the instruction of ELLs.

Safe Learning Spaces

Inclusive and safe learning spaces need to be created for all English learners, an often vulnerable population of students that are at an increased risk for academic and social difficulties. In order to accomplish this task, Haynes and Zacarian (2010) suggested that *all* teachers be able to

- plan lessons according to their students' stages of second-language acquisition to ensure their instruction complements their ELL students' abilities,
- sustain low-anxiety, nonthreatening class environments and assign meaningful tasks to help ELLs optimally engage in learning,
- explicitly instruct ELLs in academic language, literacy learning, and American cultural norms,
- provide ELLs frequent opportunities to interact with their peers, and
- create learning spaces in which ELLs' personal and cultural experiences are embraced by all members of the class.

In addition to creating safe learning environments for students, spaces for professional learning and teacher collaboration that support teachers in their efforts to work together can also make a significant difference. Designated spaces for teamwork where resources and appropriate technology are available send the message that collaborative work is envisioned, valued, and appreciated.

TRANSFER TO PRACTICE

To address the many challenging issues that are often presented to us about collaborative teaching, we will draw from authentic questions we have been asked over the past seven years concerning the practices of collaboration and co-teaching. These questions often involve the timeframes for instructional conversations, the scheduling of co-taught classes, the management of shared spaces, and the best way to establish a successful collaborative, integrated service delivery model for the sake of ELLs. And many of the answers require out-of-the-box thinking.

Getting Started

A question we get asked most frequently is of a very general nature: What is the most essential first step toward starting a successful collaborative teaching model in a school? Whether your collaborative teaching is conducted in the same class—co-teaching—or in separate classrooms—parallel instruction—invariably our answer is always: Start small. Although some school leaders roll out a new initiative in a grand way to include all faculty and classes, unless generous amounts of time are provided for planning, organization, professional learning, and teacher buy-in, the proposed initiative most likely will get off to a rocky start. Danielson (2007) maintained that many school leaders simply do not have the time to concentrate on school improvement and the demands of leadership—maintaining a sense of vision, managing day-to-day building needs, acting as instructional leader, being accountable to federal, state, and community demands. Moreover, other concerns often prevent administrators from remaining focused on improvement initiatives.

Our idea of starting small simply means to foster the enthusiasm of a small group of teachers who are interested in the new initiative—in this case, collaborative teaching—for which a pilot program is established. School leaders ask for teachers to volunteer and have willing teachers speak to potential teaching partners to encourage others to participate. If an administrator does not have enough teachers to volunteer, teachers who already work well with ELLs should be asked to take part. Although these selected teachers may have been "voluntold," a school leader's confidence in their expertise will encourage their buy-in.

The grade level or subject area to build a collaboratively taught program will depend on the needs of individual schools. Some elementary administrators may choose classes or grades that have a higher concentration of ELLs, while secondary administrators may focus on a particular content area for collaboration or co-teaching, such as English language arts. We have observed successfully run co-taught classes at the secondary level in many different subjects—mathematics, science, and social studies as well as English language arts. The subject matter is not as important as the willingness and expertise of the teachers who are teaching it.

Foster teacher leadership by having established teacher teams plan and organize the pilot program. Invite educators in the field who are knowledgeable about collaborative teaching to work with your teachers through professional learning sessions and instructional coaching. Encourage your teams to engage in book studies, webinars, and other avenues of learning on the topic. During the first year, there will be much exploration and experimentation with what works and what does not. Have teachers document their successes and challenges with collaborative teaching, and at the end of the year, showcase the pilot program to your faculty.

Building Collaborative Teacher Teams

A common practice is to develop a core partnership that includes a classroom or content teacher and an ESL teacher. This combination provides the backbone for the co-teaching or collaborative team. In order to nurture the partnership, we recommend the following:

- Establish regular avenues of communication from the outset in order for the core team to practice ongoing collaborative activities.
- Identify leadership roles and individual responsibilities.
- Outline decision-making strategies such as which decisions can be made individually and which should be made in consultation with one another.
- Review available co-teaching models and make decisions as to whether lessons will be conducted in the same or separate classroom settings. (Honigsfeld & Dove, 2010a, p. 95)

Other faculty such as literacy or special education teachers can provide additional support for collaborative teaching depending upon students' learning needs in individual classes.

Paraprofessionals such as teacher assistants, classroom aides, and bilingual support staff can be an important part of a collaborative team. These staff members may have practical knowledge of individual students' academic, language, and social skills. In addition, school leaders may choose to participate in regular collaborative team meetings.

Flexible configurations of teacher teams foster ongoing collaboration and continuous, planned opportunities for teachers and administrators to engage in meaningful dialogue about instruction and student learning. Whether teachers are engaged in co-teaching ELLs, in-class coaching, mentoring new teachers, reciprocal classroom observations, or specific teacher study groups to increase understanding of ELLs, varying teacher groups is essential for continuous collaboration. Some alternative team groupings are as follows:

- *Grade-level planning teams:* General education and ESL teachers are the core members who may be joined by literacy specialists, speech pathologists, special education teachers, and other faculty or support staff. These teams may meet daily or weekly to discuss core curriculum, planning, and student assessment data and work to facilitate co-teaching for ELLs.

- *Content area planning teams:* ESL teachers meet on a weekly or monthly basis with specialists segregated by subject (English language arts, mathematics, science, social studies) to align curriculum and standards for ELLs and share instructional strategies in their areas of expertise.

- *Cross-grade planning teams:* The main focus of multigrade team meetings is for all teachers to be aware of grade-level expectations both above and below their curriculum level and to better understand the demands of upcoming standardized assessments for ELLs. Cross-grade planning may occur once per month or at specific intervals throughout the school year.

- *ESL planning teams:* ESL specialists meet weekly or biweekly to discuss their successes and challenges with co-teaching, meeting curricular demands, specific issues regarding student learning difficulties, and the use of innovations and techniques with English learners. (Honigsfeld & Dove, 2010b, pp. 115–116)

School leaders who value collaborative practices uncover innovative ways to arrange team meetings in schedules that are already overburdened. Nevertheless, a clear-cut plan for deliberate, ongoing meetings is vital for a school community to engage in dialogue in the most meaningful ways. Table 5.1 illustrates the key components of an ongoing collaboration framework.

Scheduling

One of the major hurdles of organizing a co-taught program is scheduling. School leaders and teachers often ask, How do you effectively schedule a co-teaching program for the sake of English learners across the grade levels in a whole school? The answer to this question requires program clarity through decision making, organization, and examination of available resources. Consider the following:

- Identify the ideal amount of time an ESL teacher should spend co-teaching weekly in classes with his or her students. Some states allow individual school districts to make this determination while others have mandated a set amount of time per week that should be designated for ESL instruction.

Table 5.1 Framework for Ongoing Collaboration

Steps to take	Essential elements for consideration
Identify the participants	• Grade-level teams • Content area teams • Interdisciplinary teams
Set the purpose	• Data review • Lesson planning • Material adaptation • Reflection • Student learning • Study of specific content • Sharing strategies and best practices
Establish required time frame and scheduling logistics	• Before or after school • Scheduled congruence period • Lunchtime • Online
Determine needed resources	• Shared values • Supportive leadership • Protocols for conversation

- Consider the number of ESL teachers on staff and if you have an adequate number to reach all of your English learners solely through a co-taught program. If you have one ESL teacher who is responsible for eighty ELLs across five grade levels, co-teaching for all classes will not be feasible.
- Facilitate the formation of co-taught classes by clustering ELLs so that they are assigned to fewer classes. Instead of placing a few English learners in every grade level or content area class, consider designating one class per grade level. (*See more information about student clustering in this chapter.*)
- Examine the possibilities for a combination of a co-taught ESL and pullout/lab program model to reach the needs of more students.

With scheduling, out-of-the-box thinking is critical in order to use available resources most effectively. In cases where staffing is an issue, be selective about which classes are co-taught.

Some schools have a combination of a co-taught program and pullout or stand-alone classes for English language instruction. For part of the designated instructional time, the ESL teacher co-teaches in a grade level or content class alongside the classroom teacher, and the rest of the time is spent in a separate ESL class or language lab. Table 5.2 is an example of one possible schedule for an elementary school ESL teacher.

In the sample elementary schedule (Table 5.2), there is a heavier concentration of co-teaching in first, second, and third grades. The decision to schedule more co-taught sessions in one grade rather than another is generally due to a higher concentration of English learners in a particular class. Other considerations include an individual teacher's ability to communicate, build partnerships, and commit to the collaborative teaching process.

To accommodate the teaching of a greater number of children and classes, co-taught lessons are paired with an ESL lab period where students are pulled for additional instruction, most often pre-teaching or re-teaching information, strategies, or skills that will be or were developed in the grade-level class. These back-to-back scheduled periods might also be adjusted to accommodate double periods of co-teaching in some classes on a rotating basis. To facilitate co-teaching, some administrators adjust teachers' class schedules across a grade level so that the subject being taught varies from class to class. In this way, an ESL teacher

Table 5.2 ESL Teaching Schedule: Elementary

	Monday	**Tuesday**	**Wednesday**	**Thursday**	**Friday**
Period 1	Grade 1 co-teaching	Grade 5 co-teaching	Grade 1 co-teaching	Grade 5 co-teaching	Grade 1 co-teaching
Period 2	Grades 1 & 2 ESL lab (pullout)	Grades 4 & 5 ESL lab	Grades 1 & 2 ESL lab (pullout)	Grades 4 & 5 ESL lab	Grades 1 & 2 ESL lab (pullout)
Period 3	Grade 2 co-teaching	Grade 4 co-teaching	Grade 2 co-teaching	Grade 4 co-teaching	Grade 2 co-teaching
Period 4	Grade 3 co-teaching	Grade 3 co-teaching	Grade 3 co-teaching	Grade 1 co-teaching	Grade 3 co-teaching
Period 5	Grade 3 ESL lab	Grade 3 ESL lab	Grade 3 ESL lab	Grade 1 ESL lab	Grade 3 ESL lab
Period 6	Lunch	Lunch	Lunch	Lunch	Lunch
Period 7	Grades 4 & 5 ESL lab	Grade 1 co-teaching	Grades 4 & 5 ESL lab	Grade 2 co-teaching	Grades 4 & 5 ESL lab
Period 8	Prep	Grade 1 ESL lab	Prep	Grade 2 ESL lab	Prep

will have more opportunities to co-teach in classes on the same grade level and in the same subject area, but at a different time during the day.

Similarly, Table 5.3 outlines a sample secondary ESL teacher schedule. In this schedule, the ESL teacher is assigned to co-teach in the core subject areas of English language arts and mathematics, and time is also designated for stand-alone ESL classes to meet various student needs.

We often advise administrators in secondary schools to schedule co-taught classes first. It not only can facilitate the arrangement of common planning time for the co-teachers but also clearly identifies that this population of students is important.

Learning Lab

vs. SH?

Table 5.3 ESL Teaching Schedule: Secondary

	High School ESL Co-Teaching/Lab Schedule Monday–Friday
Period 1	English language arts—Grade 9—Co-teaching
Period 2	ESL lab—Grades 9 and 10
Period 3	English language arts—Grade 10—Co-teaching
Period 4	Mathematics—Grade 11—Co-teaching
Period 5	Professional learning—Interdisciplinary team meeting
Period 6	Lunch
Period 7	ESL lab—Grades 11 and 12
Period 8	Preparation and planning

What Research Says:

Robert Canady and Michael Rettig (1995) noted,

Fragmented instructional time is an issue at all levels. In elementary school, a variety of practices contribute to this problem. For example, haphazardly scheduled pullout programs (for ESL or special education, for example) disrupt classroom instruction; and because the schedules of specialists (for music and art, for example) are created for periods of varying length, core teachers must plan instruction around the remaining chopped-up time. . . . At the middle and high school levels, fragmentation occurs in a different way. Students traveling through a six-, seven-, or eight-period day encounter the same number of pieces of unconnected curriculum each day, with little opportunity for in-depth study. (p. 4)

Class Configuration and Student Clustering

The idea of carefully configuring classes so that English learners are assigned to fewer of them is a straightforward concept to increase the contact time an ESL teacher will have with students in various grade-level or content area classes. However, keep in mind that merely placing English learners in clusters to facilitate teacher collaboration or a co-taught schedule is not enough. For this practice to be most effective, the classroom or content teacher should have the knowledge of how to work with this population of youngsters even when the ESL co-teacher is not present. In addition, all teachers should be able to build a class community in which variations of language abilities, cultural norms, and academic skills are welcomed.

Without a doubt, there is much to be done to develop an understanding of the practice of student clustering among school community members, and its practice should not be attempted without thoughtful consideration as to whether it will bring about the perceived benefits. In smaller schools with fewer English learners, school leaders must avoid the appearance of segregating students. Moreover, all teachers and administrators should be secure in the knowledge that ELLs are a heterogeneous group of learners comprised of a wide range of academic abilities and varying levels of literacy.

School leaders must carefully create ELL placement policies and be mindful of their implications. One possible way to cluster ELLs is to base class assignments on the local population and demographics. Saint Paul Public Schools (SPPS) uses the following formula in order to cluster their English learners:

- Assign ELLs in one or two classrooms when less than 30 percent of students are ELLs.
- Cluster, but be sure ELLs do not exceed 50 percent of any class roster, when 30 to 50 percent of students are ELLs.
- Distribute ELLs among all classrooms but group by need or language level when 50 percent or more of students are ELLs.

Fearon (2008) reported a similar ratio developed for a team teaching pilot program in a New Jersey public school, in which the number of ELLs did not exceed nine students or 50 percent of the class. All in all, administrators must consider placing English learners in classes with teachers who are highly competent in their knowledge and skills concerning second-language acquisition, cultural understandings, and teaching methods and techniques, and who demonstrate the professional dispositions and positive attitudes toward linguistically and culturally diverse student populations.

Time and Space for Sustained, Meaningful Professional Interactions

Both time and space are factors in determining the successful implementation of a collaborative model of teaching. For this reason, scheduling collaborative practices must begin with identifying an overall purpose for professional conversations and determining how they might best be had. Additionally, the necessary resources to provide the time and space for teacher collaboration needs to be considered for any long-term plan. In any case, a schoolwide commitment to collaborative practices is paramount.

Leadership Voice From the Field

David Forker, ESOL (English for Speakers of Other Languages) Specialist/Title III, Clarke County School District, Athens, Georgia, emphasizes the importance of norms and routines for communication:

> It is imperative for teachers to able to communicate with each other effectively. To that end, we have found that it is tremendously important for our teacher teams to acknowledge the differences among communicating, collaborating, and co-teaching, and have focused conversations about how they will communicate with each other prior to beginning their work collaborating or co-teaching. Districtwide, we have found that the time our teacher teams spend establishing communicative and collaborative norms prior to initiating their work together paves the way for them to be able to communicate and collaborate in order to co-teach our English learners as effectively as possible. (personal communication, July 24, 2014)

Several obstacles can challenge teachers who want to engage in professional conversations, the most significant one being a lack of time to coordinate essential conversations concerning lesson planning, material adaptation, student data, and so on for a well-run collaborative model of teaching. When administrators offer teachers time for collaboration, these discussions may occur at the end of the school day, when teachers are tired from their day's work and may not be as productive. For this reason, having time during the school day can increase teacher enthusiasm and participation in the process. Table 5.4 suggests ways to facilitate scheduled time for collaborative teams to meet.

Collaborative instruction and co-teaching also necessitate that educators share work areas both inside and outside of the classroom. Teachers may also share virtual spaces in the form of online and networked tools for ongoing professional discourse. Some school leaders designate a particular

Table 5.4 Creating Opportunities for Teachers to Meet During the School Day

Key practices	How to achieve them

Adjust school schedules	• Establish one period per week, at the beginning or end of the school day, in which students are engaged on the playground or in the auditorium so teachers can meet.
	• Devise a common planning period for teachers.
	   o Employ substitute teachers to cover classes.
	   o Reduce the number of periods teachers have contact with students.
	   o Schedule special subjects (art, music, etc.) during same time block.
	• Modify the school schedule to add 15 minutes per day for four days with early dismissal on day five, leaving one hour each week for collaboration.

Provide incentives	• Provide extra pay for teachers who formally collaborate during their lunchtime. • Employ school aides to release teachers from lunch or recess duty. • Offer teachers rewards; for example, for the first to obtain the latest technology or for collaborating during personal preparation time.
Use resources more efficiently	• Have certain teachers (literacy, gifted and talented, etc.) provide special lessons in classrooms to free up general education teachers. • Redistribute students for one period so that three classes become two. • Invite community members to demonstrate their talents for students to free up teachers. • Consider funding sources and available grant money to fund a collaboration initiative.
Find time during class hiatus	• Employ staff development days for teaching teams to conduct long-term planning. • Increase the number of days teachers work or decrease the number of days school is in session. • Use faculty meetings before and after school. • Engage students in community service or in-school tutoring for younger pupils to free teachers to meet.

room or work area that is specified for collaborative teamwork. These spaces are often equipped with comfortable seating, professional libraries, and the basic technology for teams to plan instruction, review data, study new ideas, and reflect on teaching practices.

To foster the sharing of physical and virtual spaces, building leaders can do the following:

- Create inviting, functional, professional rooms as places for teacher collaboration, including spaces for small- and large-group meetings
- Establish and continuously update the school's professional library, where teacher resources may be accessed, examined, and discussed
- Support and promote virtual spaces—Dropbox, Google docs, or other district-selected platforms—for teachers to share their lesson plans, teacher-created instructional materials, and assessment tools

Collaborative Program Feasibility

In order to sustain a collaborative model of instruction for ELLs, adequate staffing to meet the needs of the number of planned collaborative or co-taught classes needs to be in place. For example, if you have thirty classes with English learners and only three ESL teachers, most likely you will not be able to maintain a collaborative program on a large scale. In cases like these, classes for collaborative teaching will have to be strategically selected. In some school districts, administrators determine the program of instruction for ELLs depending on students' language proficiency. For instance, newcomers who speak little or no English might be in self-contained ESL classes, intermediate-level students in co-taught classes, and advanced-level students in mainstream or content classes that feature sheltered instruction. In low-incidence districts where there are few ESL students who are spread across numerous buildings, the ESL teacher may act as consultant teacher to assist classroom teachers with instruction. Above all, consult state guidelines and mandates for the instruction of ELLs before embarking on any new program.

EXPANDING SHARED KNOWLEDGE AND COLLABORATIVE LEADERSHIP PRACTICES

The following resources and collaborative professional activities are designed to support your efforts as an administrator and instructional leader to establish the foundations for collaborative, integrated ESL/ELD programs.

Key Resources

- Peterson, K. (with R. Brietzke). (1994). *Building collaborative cultures: Seeking ways to reshape urban schools.* Retrieved from http://www.ncrel.org/sdrs/areas/issues/educatrs/leadrshp/le0pet.htm
- Ferguson, C. (2005). *Developing a collaborative team approach to support family and community connections with schools: What can school leaders do?* Retrieved from http://www.sedl.org/connections/resources/rb/research-brief3.pdf
- Must reads from *Kappan*, 2010–2011: Working together [Special issue]. *Phi Delta Kappan*, Summer issue 1.
- Web 2.0 Cool Tools for Schools: Virtual Learning Spaces and Collaborative Tools: http://cooltoolsforschools.wikispaces.com/Collaborative+Tools

Activities for Professional Learning

1. Examine the following figure adapted from Kohm and Nance (2009).

When there is cooperative decision making . . .	When there are administrative directives . . .
Teachers provide feedback to their peers by examining each others instructional plans	Teachers are reluctant to explore ideas beyond what is being asked
Teachers jointly take risks, examine outcomes, and reflect on their practice together	Teachers don't look for instructional solutions; they keep the status quo or expect school leaders to resolve issues
Teachers share their successes with each other and build on one another's ideas	Individual teachers have isolated successes that do not affect overall student achievement
Teachers work together to develop instructional activities that will lead students to meet learning benchmarks	Ideas are often limited due to the beliefs that "if it ain't broke, don't fix it"

SOURCE: Kohm and Nance, (2009, p. 67).

Engage your faculty in a discussion about the value of a collaborative school culture. Have teachers work in teams to identify examples in their practice of the items on the chart. Determine what elements of a collaborative school culture are present in your school and what might need to change.

2. David Piercey (2010) asserted, "Collaboration may simply mean different things to different people. Without making our assumptions clear, we may never fully understand each other's meaning" (p. 55). At a faculty meeting, give teachers an opportunity to share their own understanding of collaboration. Have each teacher complete a simple organizer in which they define collaboration, identify its challenges, give examples from their own practice, and determine what collaboration is not (nonexamples) as follows:

Define	Challenges	Examples	Nonexamples

Provide teachers with the opportunity to share their completed organizers with various faculty members. Come to a consensus as to what the expectation for teacher collaboration should be.

3. In collaboration with members of your faculty, identify all the challenges they face related to the logistics of collaboration. Invite creative, out-of-the box solutions to these challenges and create the opportunities for piloting those solutions. If you find teacher unions may become a roadblock to successful implementation of ideas and teacher creativity, explore ways to secure union support when trying to make changes.

6 What Type of Professional Learning Is Needed to Work With ELLs Effectively?

When you are thirsty, it is too late to think about digging a well.

—Japanese proverb

Craig Gfeller, Principal, West Gate Elementary, Prince William County Schools, Virginia, showcases his success with collaborative learning teams in his school:

> *Collaboration between classroom teachers and specialists is paramount to ensuring that our English language learners achieve at their highest potential. At our school, our focus has been on creating a culture that embraces teacher collaboration as a way of guaranteeing that, regardless of which teacher is instructing our students, they get the highest quality instruction, best practices are used, and English language techniques are implemented with fidelity. This collaboration between teachers has to be intentional. Therefore, our focus has been on using specific protocols to structure collaborative learning team (CLT) meetings to make certain*

that every teacher has a voice, has clarity about the curriculum, contributes ideas to help our students learn, and knows how students will be assessed. Our vision for the school is to be a model for our county for what collaborative practices should look like and sound like among educational professionals in order to maximize student learning and achievement. (personal communication, June 4, 2014)

ESSENTIAL KNOWLEDGE

Educational leaders involved in professional development (PD) planning sometimes miss the mark when it comes to creating opportunities for learning. Often enough, they rely on resources outside their own school community to bring PD to their faculty and staff only to be sidetracked by budget cuts and other financial woes. These monetary concerns cause some leaders to either select a limited number of teachers for training or abandon their plans altogether, leaving teachers to their own devices.

According to Learning Forward's (2011) Standards of Professional Learning, "The most powerful forms of professional development occur in ongoing communities of learners that meet on a regular basis . . . to advance the achievement of school and school system goals for student learning" (p. 5). In a similar way, Sparks (2005) contended that principals, armed with the knowledge that collaborative practices yield successful professional development results, create collegial, school-based teams as a plan for professional learning. Additionally, Darling-Hammond and Richardson (2009) determined that collaborative practices via a learning community model were the most successful for professional learning purposes. So why do school leaders hesitate to form learning teams to develop strategies for teaching English language learners (ELLs)? The answer is often due to the perceived mystery behind the education of linguistically diverse students.

In spite of the research, even proactive school administrators question which staff development activities yield the most success for their teachers and other members of the school community to understand the challenges of ELLs to achieve academically. This concern for effective professional development has never been timelier for those school leaders involved with adapting instruction for ELLs to meet new, rigorous learning standards. More than ever before, administrators are impelled to provide useful teaching strategies for teachers of ELLs and to investigate instructional materials and technology with the hope of satisfying learning benchmarks and positively affecting ELLs' academic achievement. Yet according to Michael Fullan (2011), building and leading a collaborative school culture is key to bring about successful improvements in school organizations.

Often enough, because the topic concerns English learners, an area of instruction that confounds administrators and teachers alike, the impulse is often to seek outside experts.

Certainly there are positive outcomes from the use of professional developers to provide faculty with teaching techniques and English-building activities for the benefit of multilingual learners. We frequently present workshops throughout the country on strategies for teaching ELLs. However, the main focus of our presentations is on building capacity through collaborative practices and developing a collaborative school culture for the sake of ELLs. Newly learned instructional strategies generally cannot be fully developed and are not sustainable without some type of ongoing internal instructional support.

To this end, we would like to dispel the mystery of ELL instruction and reveal the most important elements principals and other administrators must invest in—strategies to develop collaborative instructional practices within school communities with ELLs in mind, and to a smaller degree, traditional, outside resources for professional development. For the most part, leaders already have the knowledge and skills within their own school communities just waiting to unfold in their own backyard.

Professional Development Needs of Instructional Faculty

What Research Says:

In addition, in spite of the ineffectiveness of short-term and whole-school professional development activities, these kinds of programs remain ubiquitous in schools. Mandated professional development activities—in which administrators select the topics and teachers are a captive audience for a half or whole day—are notoriously unproductive. The result is often frustration and resentment on the part of teachers, dissatisfaction on the part of administrators, and a fruitless allocation of scarce resources. (Nieto, 2009, p. 9)

Conventional practices of faculty learning are giving way to more contemporary and effective models of staff development, which consist of opportunities for educators to pursue individual inquiries, learn skills and techniques from peers, engage in action research, or explore curriculum and instructional initiatives (Joyce & Calhoun, 2010). "In addition to refining education in their own classrooms, teachers' research can contribute local evidence to discussions about educational policies in their schools and districts" (Cazden, 2001, p. 181).

Teachers must also share in the planning of their own professional development (Sparks & Hirsh, 1997). To capitalize on collaborative practices for professional learning, various steps must be taken to ensure that the assessed needs of both students and faculty are carefully matched with professional development that accomplishes overall objectives.

Professional development considerations. Before initiating a professional development plan that helps teachers furnish ELLs with optimum instruction and academic support, consider the following:

- What are the assessed needs of your current English learners?
- What do teachers want to know and need to know?
- Which traditional and collaborative models of professional development will optimally provide faculty members with pertinent techniques and skills for assisting ELLs?
- How might leaders differentiate professional development for novice and experienced teachers? For English-as-a-second-language (ESL) or English language development (ELD) specialists, classroom teachers, and all other school personnel?

The most effective way to answer these questions and to plan and initiate effective professional development is through the collaboration of all parties concerned and charged with the education of ELLs (Rubin, 2009). Administrators can establish collaborative efforts by doing the following:

1. Have groups of teachers and administrators collaboratively review available assessment data, class work, and homework of ELLs.

2. Jointly draw conclusions concerning what areas of study ELLs need to develop, and identify the teaching skills that are necessary to assist them.

3. Engage teachers in determining ways to acquire identified techniques and strategies for teaching ELLs. Challenge teachers to explore innovative, alternative ways they may not have previously considered for acquiring new information.

4. Present information through collaborative professional development models (see *Effective Professional Development Practices* in this chapter).

5. Invite teachers to offer input regarding their personal learning goals and feedback on how professional development might be geared toward their level of expertise.

The importance of professional development that supports instruction for ELLs has been further documented by a large-scale study that examined leadership variables in five states as they relate to ELLs and services for them. Rivera et al. (2010) concluded that

> not surprisingly, principals identified professional development and effective instructional strategies as the factors that contributed the most to their ELLs' successful academic performance. At the core of contemporary dialogue on education, these factors emerged repeatedly as principals analyzed contributing dynamics and identified examples of effective practices at their schools. Access to high-quality professional development enables teachers to examine alternatives to their teaching methods and familiarize themselves with updated materials, in addition to augmenting their content knowledge and confidence. Simultaneously, the use of effective research-based strategies validates instructional methodologies, facilitates data collection, and eliminates the uncertainty of testing new teaching methods. (p. 24)

COLLEGE AND CAREER READINESS STANDARDS AND PROFESSIONAL LEARNING

Rigorous state standards in English language arts and mathematics establish what students should know and be able to do but do not provide the guidance as to how schools can help ELLs meet these standards. To this end, school districts will need to support their programs for ELLs. Some specific areas of development and learning for members of the school community to address during staff development activities are as follows:

- Establishing a formalized curriculum for ELL programs and aligning them with mainstream curricula using state standards
- Incorporating the foundational skills in reading and mathematics for middle and high school programs with beginning-level ELLs in order to build their basic facility with literacy and numeracy in English before secondary grade-level standards are addressed and met
- Promoting the shared expertise of ESL/ELD and literacy specialists with classroom and content area teachers to support all efforts to develop ELLs' grade-level reading and writing skills in history/social studies, science, and technical subjects
- Investigating multilevel resources in order to expose ELLs to a balance between informational and literary texts

- Adapting and scaffolding content so that it is made accessible to support ELLs arguments, opinions, and conclusions with evidence from texts in both their conversations and in their writing
- Developing quality questioning techniques to help all students learn, analyze, evaluate, and reflect on text-related information
- Employing a variety of strategies to teach ELLs academic vocabulary

Professional Learning for ESL/ELD and Bilingual Specialists

Various local, state, national, and international organizations sponsor conferences and workshops throughout the school year that present up-to-date information to both teachers and administrators about the education of ELLs. Administrators may assume that these ESL/bilingual symposia are primarily for ESL/bilingual faculty to yield professional betterment. However, generally speaking, both novice and experienced ESL and bilingual faculty often improve their teaching skills from varied staff development opportunities that may *not* be fully addressed at ESL/bilingual conferences.

Content-based ESL/ELD—the development of English language skills through the use of subject-area topics, information, and vocabulary—is a widely accepted contemporary method of instruction for ELLs (Echevarria, Vogt, & Short, 2010) and well supported by English language proficiency standards set by Teachers of English to Speakers of Other Languages (TESOL, 2006). However, ESL and bilingual teachers frequently do not have the necessary K–12 content area expertise to more fully support the specific academic learning of ELLs. Therefore, these specialists would be better able to enhance their teaching repertoire by collaboratively attending workshops and seminars or jointly participating in teacher study groups or collegial circles on developing their own content area literacy, increasing their own understanding of all core subject matter curricula, and learning about adapting subject-specific content in science, math, or social studies to various levels of language proficiencies.

Another strong argument for why ESL/ELD and bilingual teachers should be given the opportunity to develop content area knowledge is so they may better participate in collaborative practices, which include joint planning, co-developing materials, collaboratively assessing student work, and enhancing their ability to participate in co-taught lessons, if possible (Honigsfeld & Dove, 2010a). It is vital for ESL and bilingual teachers to acquire fluency and facility with content area information and skills in order to assist ELLs in meeting the Common Core State Standards (CCSS).

Professional Learning for Other School Faculty and Staff

Classroom teachers, content area specialists, and noninstructional staff will also profit greatly from participating in professional learning opportunities that target the academic, social, and emotional needs of ELLs. Some of the information and skills school faculty acquire through such professional development events include the following:

- The connection between language and culture
- The ways in which the culture of the student's home affects his or her behavior and academic progress in school
- Strategies for developing communication between the student's home and school faculty and personnel
- The reasons for incorporating the background knowledge of ELLs in lessons
- How content material (science, social studies, etc.) can be used to develop ELLs' vocabulary, reading, and writing skills
- How to make lessons more comprehensible for ELLs at all levels of proficiency
- How to modify assessment practices to ensure accurate measurements of language and academic performance

Exploring strategies for working with ELLs is essential for classroom and content area teachers, school psychologists, social workers, and all others who need to understand this particular population of youngsters to help them become actively participating, responsible members of the school community and meet academic standards.

What Research Says:

Johnson and Marx (2009) described an effective professional development program as having the following components:

(a) intensive, sustained, whole-school efforts focused on the development of student conceptual understanding through culturally relevant science and effective teaching methods which incorporate literacy and language strategies; (b) focus on building relationships between teachers and teachers, teachers and students, and teachers and university faculty members; (c) creation of positive school and classroom climate through procedures and routines for participating in science class and high expectations for success. (p. 118)

Effective Professional Development Practices

Traditional staff development often has little impact on student achievement. It tends to feature one-stop workshops that provide a great deal of information but offer teachers few if any opportunities to apply newfound knowledge or reflect on their own practices with fellow faculty members. Not only does some professional development lack connections to classroom practices, it often is not differentiated for teachers' various levels of expertise, their years of teaching experience, and their own personal preferences for learning new material. When teachers from a range of academic disciplines attend professional development together, the information they receive is congruent, and the benefit is even greater if teachers have the opportunity to reflect on their learning collectively to support one another to teach ELLs (Honigsfeld & Dove, 2010a).

Collaborative practices. Teacher collaboration must be the foundation of planning and delivering instruction for ELLs. In the same way, collaborative professional development is essential in creating effective team building among all teachers of ELLs. Some of the most important ingredients combined in successful collaborative professional development are as follows:

1. Ongoing, school-based meetings to reflect on the instruction of ELLs

2. Shared interests to meet the concerns of all team members

3. Voluntary team participation

4. Meeting points that concentrate on instructional practices and students' learning

5. Models of learning that meet the varied needs of individual participants (See Table 6.1)

Instructional coaching. With this approach, teachers can engage in collaborative conversations with an outside or in-house expert to develop specific knowledge and skills that target ELLs. Coaching provides opportunities for individualized support for teaching subject-specific classes and assists teachers in developing different methods of instruction through collaborative discussions. Teachers need to understand ELLs' unique learning challenges and their "wide variety of educational and cultural experiences . . . as well as their considerable linguistic differences" (Echevarria, Vogt, & Short, 2008, p. 7). An instructional coach with expertise in the education of ELLs can work directly with classroom teachers to collaboratively plan a course of action to increase ELLs' academic success (Dove & Colagiacomo, 2012).

Improving the one-stop workshop model. Within collaborative learning environments, external facilitators can offer an impetus for teacher engagement and learning by balancing internal and external school factors to advance teachers to higher levels of reflective practice (Easton, 2008). These types of workshops can be used as tools to gather essential information and learning resources for teachers who already have buy-in, are part of established learning communities, and are willing to take on leadership roles. Streamlining workshops to meet the needs of a specific group of teachers can be very cost effective. The one-stop workshop can be highly motivating by sparking ideas among those teachers who will take suggested resources and develop ideas through collaborative efforts. In this way, professional development can be tailored to meet the specific needs of those concerned and outside experts—although used sparingly—can make a greater impact.

Administrative participation is of the utmost importance. In addition to the format, administrators must be active leaders and collaborators in the staff development practices of their faculty. Genuine collaboration requires the engagement of decision makers. School building leaders need to have firsthand knowledge of the information, applications, and reflections generated by their school's professional development participants through direct involvement in the process. Principals and other building leaders must attend workshops, participate in research development, and have opportunities for faculty and staff to offer their feedback through ongoing interdisciplinary meetings. For professional development to be most effective, building leaders must make sustained professional growth for everyone a priority.

Collaborative Team Learning

Apart from the reasons that collaborative professional learning is an essential framework for supporting sustained instructional practices with ELLs, what exactly do collaborative teams do? How do these teams actually work to bring about needed changes and support for classroom instruction?

Educators have their own sets of individual teaching competencies coupled with their own knowledge of the content they teach. What collaborative team members do is share their individual competencies with one another so that they become a collective set of instructional proficiencies. Revisiting the collaborative instructional practices we presented in Chapter 3, the following are some examples of what collaborative teams do to increase their instructional capacity (Honigsfeld & Dove, 2010a):

1. **Co-planning**. An ESL teacher and a middle-school science teacher plan lessons together. The science teacher learns teaching strategies

about how to present new information and adapt the science content for ELLs. In turn, the ESL/ELD teacher learns content-specific information and vocabulary ELLs will need to be successful in science class.

2. **Curriculum alignment.** A third-grade teacher, a literacy specialist, and an ESL teacher team up to develop a reading curriculum for a third-grade class. They cooperatively learn the new CCSS and write a curriculum that reflects the standards, meets developmental language and literacy needs, and fits the structure of a third grader's instructional day.

3. **Co-developing instructional materials.** A team of high-school social studies teachers and ESL teachers identify areas of concern in the curriculum for ELs. They collectively decide on strategies to meet these youngsters' needs and divide the workload to adapt content and find adequate resources to support the learning of their ELs.

4. **Collaborative assessment of student work.** Interdisciplinary teams of teachers examine the work of ELs to determine how to best identify their academic progress and challenges. Teachers then devise a cohesive set of strategies that are used across disciplines to meet the overall learning needs of these youngsters. Teams meet regularly to report on the progress of their students and adjust their instructional repertoires.

A Leadership Voice From the Field

Remy Rummel, Coordinator, English Language Development, K–12, Douglas County School District, Colorado:

While collaborative practices and co-teaching benefit all learners, they are critical for English language learners. Language is not acquired in isolated, preplanned time periods. Language acquisition occurs throughout the entire day, and co-teaching affords students educational experiences that simultaneously and purposefully foster content and language development. Co-teaching is instrumental in our progress toward . . . the "all teachers are teachers of language" paradigm. . . . Collaboration among teachers has ignited powerful instructional conversations; it has strengthened our professional learning communities. By first setting expectations and expressing needs, teachers co-plan throughout the backward-planning process, create and implement innovative instruction and assessment, and continuously refine instructional practice. Collaboration and co-teaching provide opportunities for teachers to empower students to exceed expectations and work toward their full potential. (personal communication, July 27, 2014)

Hirsh and Killion (2009) reminded all educators what the Nation Staff Development Council (NSDC, more recently renamed Learning Forward) has adopted as its purpose: "Every educator engages in effective professional learning every day so every student achieves. NSDC believes that without educators learning every day, the opportunity for all students to achieve is severely diminished" (p. 71).

In order to improve the quality of staff development, elsewhere Hirsh (2009) suggested school leaders develop professional learning opportunities to directly meet improvement goals by

- clearly connecting the purpose of staff development to educational outcomes,
- embedding learning into the school day through the use of learning teams,
- inviting teachers to identify and determine the course of their professional learning,
- presenting numerous opportunities for practitioners to understand, practice, and incorporate new strategies into their classroom routines, and
- providing teachers with choices regarding how they develop their own learning.

In order to enhance teacher commitment and program application, Hirsh also suggested "teacher groups . . . choose from among developing lesson plans, creating common assessments, peer observations and feedback and more" (p. 71).

TRANSFER TO PRACTICE

School leaders decidedly can influence change (Fullan, 2007), which can lead to the development of a collaborative school culture. Fullan described such leaders as "initiators or facilitators of continuous improvements . . . in the middle of the relationship between teachers and external ideas and people" (p. 155). Administrators can foster change for the sake of ELLs "by working collaboratively with faculty and staff to develop learning communities, which confer, oversee, and support the change process" (Dove & Freeley, 2011, p. 29).

Planning and Implementing Sustained Professional Development

Although administrators draw upon numerous models to plan professional development for their school members, we strongly believe that sustained collaborative models of professional learning are most productive in bring about school change. According to Joyce and Calhoun (2010),

> Teachers who think and study together can make positive changes that, moreover, can make a serious difference in student learning in a relatively short time. A change in curriculum and instruction that will make a difference to student learning begins to do so when it is implemented. (p. 62)

The first step in planning for collaborative professional development involves familiarizing the faculty with cooperative practices. The most common types of collaborative models are outlined in Table 6.1.

Table 6.1 Team Practices for Professional Development

Practice	Activities
Collegial circles	Teachers meet on a regular basis to discuss common questions, share concerns, offer solutions to common problems and appropriate instructional techniques.
Peer observations	All teachers of ELLs are provided opportunities to visit one another's classes to observe the teaching-learning process and ELL outcomes in the classroom.
Collaborative coaching and mentoring	Teachers support each other's practice through a framework of modeling effective instruction and providing ongoing, student-centered classroom assistance for one another.
Research and development	Teachers collaboratively study and review research related to an instructional approach for ELLs and plan and implement lessons based on their studies.
Collaborative inquiry (action research)	This is a more in-depth exploration of an overarching concept that deals with ELLs' language acquisition or instructional needs—also known as teacher research or action research.
Lesson study	Teachers jointly plan a lesson in response to a preestablished study question or goal. Through repeated lesson observations and discussions, teachers revise the lesson as it is re-taught and observed in each new class.
Professional-learning communities (PLCs)	PLCs create a structure for improving schools by establishing and enacting a collaborative school culture and a collective purpose for learning.

Practice	Activities
Professional-learning networks (PLNs)	PLNs take advantage of social media and function as online communities for learning.
Collaborative-learning teams (CLTs)	CLTs—through shared goals, regular meetings, and an organized approach—are vehicles for teachers to engage in professional learning focused on effective instruction.

In order to initiate collaborative professional learning, a core structure for participation needs to be established. Administrators should organize members of the school community to participate in various learning activities to address established needs or interests in cooperative-learning sessions. Building leaders should become familiar not only with the characteristics of collaborative professional development models but also with the organizational strategies for faculty and staff to participate. Table 6.2 identifies possible organizational designs for collaborative practices.

Table 6.2 Organizational Options for Collaborative Models of Professional Development

Participants	Practices	Activities
Whole school staff	Research and development	All school members delve into literature about a specified topic; teachers design their own resources alone or in small groups and share them on a specially designated school website (e-board).
School staff organized into smaller study groups	Collaborative inquiry (or variations on it, such as independent study groups, collegial circles, lesson study groups, etc.)	Individual groups set procedures typically consisting of • Identifying the issue • Examining the data • Reviewing the literature • Determining and implementing a course of action
Individual faculty volunteer to participate in partner groups	Peer observations, collaborative coaching, and mentoring	Each two-person team independently determines the focus of professional improvement.

The importance of examining school culture. In order to negotiate sustained collaborative practices, we strongly advise an assessment of your school culture in order to determine what types of sustained collaborative practices are most feasible and beneficial in your school. Among the important elements to implement and sustain effective practices to meet the instructional needs of ELLs, a collaborative school culture must encompass the following:

- Respect for diversity
- Common goals
- Input from all members of the school community
- A framework for teacher peer support
- Equitable access to high quality resources
- Administrative support

A school's culture often changes over time; new administrators, initiatives, and regulations often create opportunities and challenges that alter it. Therefore, an examination and revitalization of the culture may be necessary in order for teacher collaboration to be effectively implemented.

Effective in-house practices. Building administrators play a critical role in developing, organizing, and nurturing collaborative professional learning. Apart from selecting models of professional development, key components of professional conversations and the allotted time to have group discussions and reflection are vital to effective collaborative practices. Consider the following major components of an integrated, collaborative model for ESL/ELD service delivery to be used as a tool to assess and enhance professional learning opportunities for school staff:

- What types of interdisciplinary, cross-department (cross-specialization) conversations are teachers engaged in?
- What type of and how many common-planning opportunities do teachers have to work on curriculum and instructional materials collaboratively?
- What types of shared classroom or other collaborative instructional and peer coaching experiences do teachers have?
- What opportunities are there for individual and collaborative reflection and inquiry?
- What types of administrative support and feedback are you offering to support all levels of collaboration and to create a professional-learning community through the integrated, collaborative model to serve ELLs and improve instruction for all students?

In addition, Dr. Martina T. Wagner (Independent School District 623 English Language Supervisor, Roseville Area Schools, Minnesota) notes that an integrated, collaborative model to serve ELLs is much more sustainable in an environment that has considered the school culture and other conditions and initiatives already in place. She suggests that schools and districts customize this framework to fit their local needs, established initiatives, and desired outcomes by examining additional critical questions, such as the following:

- How does the framework align with the existing conditions of a site or district?
- What processes are considered to develop leaders and/or instructional supports?
- How are instructional coaches identified, trained and kept abreast of essential information about ELLs? (personal communication, August 11, 2014)

Creating a Learning Community

Among many others, Sergiovanni (2000) offered a leadership framework for school administrators to create a unique *culture, community,* and *personal meaning* in their schools. He also discussed five key dimensions of a professional learning community, which we have adapted to emphasize the ESL context:

1. A *learning community* in which all members of the school community are recognized as capable of learning and are deeply engaged in lifelong learning

2. A *collegial community* in which all members of the school community are meaningfully connected to each other through a carefully articulated common vision and mission and shared goals that includes ELLs

3. A *caring community* in which all members of the school community are committed to the well-being of all—both those whose lives and circumstances are secure and those who are in need of support—through sincere concern, thoughtfulness, and respect

4. An *inclusive community* in which all members of the school community are respected and linguistic, cultural, ethnic, and all other differences are accepted and valued

5. An *inquiring community* in which all members of the school community are engaged in collective inquiry and in collaborative problem solving to make sure local decisions for the sake of ELLs are made together

Embracing Technology for Professional Development

Electronic tools can support requisite learning about ELLs through participation in a variety of online resources for professional development. Electronic media can provide an avenue for educators to enhance their skills and understanding of various topics by attending courses, presentations, seminars, and workshops via webinars and websites that support online learning. Free and per-cost webinars are available through professional organizations and education-related websites where potential participants may register for upcoming, scheduled events; often on these sites, webinars are archived for viewing at any time.

Technology can provide needed information to a range of participants from the whole school to individual learners. Blogs, online communities, social networks, and video chat sites have reinterpreted communication and interaction in the twenty-first century (Langer de Ramirez, 2009) and reshaped the way continued learning is accomplished. Building leaders should take advantage of the many innovative tools available on the web, and the Internet should be used as a key resource to keep faculty and staff informed of the latest developments in standards-based instruction.

Building on Teacher Expertise and Fostering Teacher Leadership

Katzenmeyer and Moller (2001) described teacher-leaders as those who "lead beyond the classroom, identify with and contribute to a community of teacher learners and leaders, and influence others toward improved educational practice" (p. 5). Teacher leadership can have a critical function in maintaining reform initiatives to increase student achievement, and the use of shared, in-house teacher expertise can be invaluable. However, the ability of teachers to be accepted by their peers as leaders often is limited (Paulu & Winters, 1998); therefore creating a school culture in which one another's input and expertise are valued is vital. By combining efforts to affirm a positive and collaborative school culture, both teachers and administrators can create a venue to share knowledge and expertise for the sake of English learners.

A Leadership Voice From the Field

Ana Carolina Behel, ESL Facilitator and Teacher, Weeden Elementary, Florence City Schools, Alabama, discusses the impact of PLCs that support collaborative instruction for ELLs:

Research shows that when teachers engage in high-quality, focused, sustained and relevant professional learning activities designed to increase student achievement, both staff and students win. At my school, we have just completed our third year of implementation of professional learning communities. Through our interdisciplinary monthly face-to-face meetings and schoolwide online discussions using Edmodo, we have experienced a school culture shift where everyone is sharing the responsibility for the development of all students and for success. There has also been a reduction in teacher isolation and an increased understanding of effective practices for all students. As a result, my ELL students are showing greater academic gains in language acquisition and in the content areas. (personal communication, July 29, 2014)

EXPANDING SHARED KNOWLEDGE AND COLLABORATIVE LEADERSHIP PRACTICES

The following resources and collaborative professional activities are designed to support your efforts as an administrator and instructional leader to build and expand a solid knowledge base about ESL/ELD programs and to develop high-quality professional learning opportunities for teachers.

Key Resources

1. Learning Forward (2011) recently published the third iteration of *Standards for Professional Learning* (http://www.learningforward .org/standards/index.cfm). Also, consider all other resources available at www.learningforward.org as expert sources of information related to professional development.

2. Explore the following professional-organizations' resources related to ELs to enhance shared professional learning in your school community:

   - Association for Supervision and Curriculum Development: www.ascd.org
   - National Association for Bilingual Education (NABE): www .nabe.org
   - National Association for Multicultural Education (NAME): www .nameorg.org
   - National Council of Teachers of English (NCTE): www.ncte.org
   - Teachers of English to Speakers of Other Languages: www.tesol.org

3. Review critical research and practical information on the following institutions' websites:

- Alliance at Brown University: www.alliance.brown.edu/
- Mid-Continent Regional Educational Laboratory: www.mcrel .org
- National Center for Research on Evaluation, Standards, and Student Testing at UCLA: www.cse.ucla.edu
- National Clearinghouse for English Language Acquisition: www .ncela.gwu.edu
- Northwest Regional Educational Laboratory: www.nwrel.org
- WestEd: A Research, Development, and Service Agency: www .wested.org
- U.S. Department of Education, Office of English Language Acquisition: www.ed.gov/offices.OELA

4. Investigate technology tools to further professional development goals.

- Video conferencing: www.skype.com and www.oovoo.com
- Voice conferencing: www.gotomeeting.com
- Webinars: www.ascd.org, www.pbs.org/teachers/webinar and www.pdkintl.org/webinars/index.htm

Activities for Professional Learning

1. Generate a professional learning wish list by inviting subgroups of teachers (grade-level clusters, specialists, or teacher teams) to identify areas of need they have related to working with English language learners.

2. In small groups, engage teachers in a reflective discussion about past professional development practices based on McLaughlin and Talbert (2006), who noted that teachers learn best as members of communities of practice. They claimed that knowledge and skill development is especially effective when teachers have the opportunity to grow professionally in a supportive environment with the following four approaches intertwined:

   o A *knowledge-centered* approach to develop essential knowledge to be able to solve locally identified problems
   o A *learner-centered* approach to connect prior knowledge and skills to the new information presented to the teacher-learner or explored collaboratively

    ○ An *assessment-centered* approach to receive ongoing feedback, guidance and support as new content and skills are developed and implemented

    ○ A *community-centered* approach to be involved in collaborative explorations of new content and skills and to build upon each other's knowledge and skills to create new understandings and practices

3. Discuss the degree to which the eight principles of professional learning as presented by Hirsch and Killion (2009) are observable in or transferable to your school community. Wherever needed, adapt and apply these principles to professional learning in response to the needs of English language learners:

    ○ Principles shape our thoughts, words, and actions.
    ○ Diversity strengthens an organization and improves its results.
    ○ Leaders are responsible for building the capacity in individuals, teams, and organizations to be leaders and learners.
    ○ Ambitious goals lead to powerful actions and remarkable results.
    ○ Maintaining the focus of professional learning on teaching and student learning produces academic success.
    ○ Evaluation strengthens performance and results.
    ○ Communities can solve their most complex problems by tapping internal expertise.
    ○ Collaboration among educators builds shared responsibility and improves student learning.

4. Share articles regularly with your faculty. For example, try the following selection of articles we have used for whole faculty studies on the importance of oral language development:

    ○ Biemiller, A. (2003). Oral comprehension sets the ceiling on reading comprehension. *American Educator, 27*(1). Retrieved from https://www.aft.org/newspubs/periodicals/ae/spring2003/hirschsboral.cfm
    ○ Frey, N., Fisher, D., & Nelson, J. (2013). Todo tiene que ver con lo que se habla: It's all about the talk. *Kappan, 94*(6), 8–13.
    ○ Smith, D., Wilson, B., & Corbett, D. (2009). Moving beyond talk. *Educational Leadership, 66*(5), 20–25.

Invite teachers to use a simple text annotation strategy called Noticings and Wonderings, which consists of marking up the article by identifying notable information and by raising questions for faculty discussion.

5. In *Supporting and Sustaining Teachers' Professional Development: A Principal's Guide*, Marilyn Tallerico (2005) identified these five elements of adult learning:

   1. Active engagement

   2. Relevance to current challenges

   3. Integration of experience

   4. Learning-style variation

   5. Choice and self-direction

As you consider expanding or enhancing professional learning for your faculty, how would you respond to these adult learning needs?

7 What Type of Leadership Is Needed for Integrated, Collaborative Schools?

If you wish to go fast, go alone. If you wish to go far, go together!

—African proverb

M itch Pinsky, former New York City Department of Education principal, recounts his success with a schoolwide approach to collaborative services for all subgroups of learners:

> *One of my core beliefs was that the ability to promote and facilitate collaborative relationships within our school community served to enhance the culture of our building, as well as improve student outcomes. My evolving leadership behaviors supported these beliefs and influenced others to achieve results. Classroom instruction was improved by setting clear expectations, observing lessons, and coaching teachers and staff. This approach provided a framework that allowed us to build strong teams, develop leadership capacity among staff, and share responsibilities. The students in our CTT (collaborative team teaching), self-contained SPED (special education), G & T*

> *(gifted and talented), enrichment, and ELL (English language learners) concentration classes were the primary beneficiaries of our schoolwide collaborative efforts. These efforts were validated by our selection as a Collaborative Community of Practice, which allowed our school to serve as a visitation site for representatives of schools throughout NYC (New York City). My selection as a 2009 Cahn Fellow at Columbia University was based, in part, on our above-mentioned efforts. I took a great deal of personal satisfaction in knowing that best practices developed in our school were adapted and integrated into other school communities.* (personal communication, July 22, 2014)

At a general meeting in a small suburban school, the faculty and administrator sat in a broad circle. At the start, the principal reviewed the professional development (PD) activities that recently took place in the district, and he asked his faculty to offer feedback about the session they attended. Faculty members took turns expressing their thoughts and feelings regarding the previous day's workshop.

One teacher reported that it was not a workshop but a lecture. Another teacher described how administrators were carefully watching in order to identify teachers who were not paying attention—how uncomfortable that made her feel! Others expressed the view that this particular session was a waste of their time. And one teacher was particularly vocal about how she thought the planning for the event was "ill conceived" because it was scheduled right before the state mathematics assessment.

In the midst of all this direct and critical talk, the behavior of the principal was quite extraordinary. During each teacher's comments, this building leader listened attentively. He did not try to explain, condone, or clarify the reasons for the PD. He did not attempt to pacify or soothe his faculty. He did not take offense or feel the need to take control of the situation. Instead, he let the teachers do the talking. He paid careful attention to what each of them had to say and in turn made them feel that what they had to say was important. His actions alone spoke volumes.

ESSENTIAL KNOWLEDGE

Supportive leadership is vital for a collaborative school community. When we consider the principal's behavior at the faculty meeting, it was undoubtedly consistent and clear; it fostered an environment in which the teachers could be direct and forthcoming about their thoughts, feelings, and ideas. And the ability to engage in honest talk—whether it is about how teachers best engage in professional learning, how to improve the school, or any other topic that requires a genuine and authentic exchange of ideas—is a strong contributing factor to a positive school culture.

What Constitutes a Positive School Culture?

Muhammad (2009) recognized that the "interaction of social, economic, parental, and political forces with the experiences and world views of educators and students creates a complex school culture that is difficult to transform" (p. 28). He observed a clash of paradigms in most schools he visited and noted the existence of four distinct groups of educators:

- The Believers maintain that all students can learn and that as educators they have a direct impact on student outcomes.
- The Fundamentalists are opposed to all reform initiatives and actively work on impeding them. They are frequently in conflict with the Believers.
- The Tweeners find themselves between the Believers and the Fundamentalists. They tend to be new to the school and devote much of their time to understanding the local norms.
- The Survivors seem to be burned out and barely meet their daily responsibilities. They merely survive as all they can attend to is their own emotional well-being.

In order to transform school culture, Muhammad (2009) suggests overcoming this type of staff division through a collective focus on learning and establishing a shared goal.

On the basis of demands placed upon students, teachers, and school administrators, we concur with Deal and Peterson (1999) regarding their research and analysis of a positive school climate. They found that schools with a strong, positive school culture were not only safe and secure places for all to learn but shared a common set of norms and values and demonstrated success in the following areas:

- Fostering effort and productivity
- Improving collegial and collaborative activities that in turn promote better communication and problem solving
- Supporting successful change and improvement efforts
- Building commitment and helping students and teachers identify with the school
- Amplifying energy and motivation of staff members and students
- Focusing attention and daily behavior on what is important and valued (pp. 7–8)

Prominent among Deal and Peterson's (1999) findings are the benefits of collaborative practices, a shared commitment to school improvement efforts, and a special focus on the diverse school population. Similarly, based on an extensive meta-analysis of studies on successful school leadership, Marzano, Waters, and McNulty (2005) established that a school leader has at least 21 responsibilities that can impact student achievement.

In order to build a purposeful community from which a strong leadership team can be created, Marzano et al. (2005) narrowed the list to nine items that are the most essential. The short list included acting as the optimizer, offering affirmation, sharing ideals and beliefs, demonstrating situational awareness, having visibility, building relationships, enhancing communication, shaping culture, and providing input. Comparing these nine items to Deal and Peterson's (1999) work, we conclude that building a culture—meaningfully creating shared values, norms, and beliefs—that "positively influences teachers, who, in turn, positively influence students" (Marzano et al., 2005, p. 47), is most likely one of the fundamental challenges and responsibilities that a school leader will face.

In sum, it has been well established that a collaborative school culture is a result of shared responsibility and shared leadership, which are equally intertwined with having collaborative classrooms (the microcultures of schooling) and a culture of collaboration in the larger educational community (the macroculture of schooling). School culture as a separate entity is nestled between the unique culture of each classroom and the unique culture of each community.

Community-Based Assets

It has been well established that principals in effective schools for ELLs foster meaningful connection between the school and ELLs and their families. The cultural, linguistic, and human capital that diverse communities bring to the school is viewed as an asset rather than a problem to solve or a barrier to overcome. Parent engagement (as opposed to parent involvement) has been distinguished as something done *with* the parents and not *to* the parents.

Ferguson (2005) suggested school leaders begin by determining the status of the school-family relationship—examining the current aspects that either encourage or discourage collaborative discourse and engagement between families and the school. He concluded that strong school leaders were able to reduce the factors that deter parent-school collaboration while increasing family and community connections. From the research, Ferguson identified the following positive influences for building family friendly schools:

- Alleviating language barriers
- Creating flexible meeting schedules so more parents can attend

- Arranging transportation for school meetings and events
- Being mindful whether or not parents feel welcome and valued

Other strategies to foster school-community relations included developing the skills of faculty and staff to be active listeners, devising school policies that advocate for family-school interactions, and promoting a positive and inclusive school culture that sustains the participation of all members of the school community.

What Research Says:

On the basis of their case study of two successful, visionary leaders for ELLs, Theoharis and O'Toole (2011) described the complexities of creating an inclusive school:

> With their social justice vision for educating ELLs, the leaders collaboratively planned and delivered inclusive ELL services. This meant the principal, general education teachers, ESL teachers, bilingual paraprofessionals, and other school personnel had to learn new skills and new roles. This required time for meetings and for collaborative planning of instruction as well as sustained professional development. Developing an inclusive approach to ELL required a concerted effort to deepen home–school connections with ELL families and a focused plan and implementation of home language support for ELLs at school. (p. 679)

Collaborative-Leadership Model

Glanz (2006) introduced a three-phase collaborative-leadership model for whole-school improvement, which was designed to serve as a framework for a collaborative approach to leading a school. An adapted version of this framework is in Figure 7.1, which identifies the three phases as (1) team building, (2) collaborative inquiry, and (3) shared decision making. We applied this framework to a schoolwide approach to collaborative service delivery for the sake of ELLs. The principal as instructional leader and lead learner and the entire school faculty and staff as sustainers engage in a range of collaborative practices as they move through the three phases. The arrows in the diagram indicate an open feedback loop between and among the three phases allowing for adjustments to plans and corrections of courses of action. The main characteristics of the three phases are indicated.

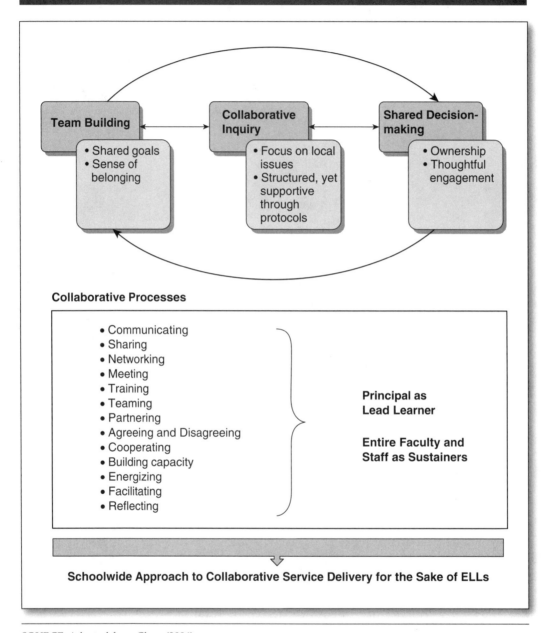

Figure 7.1 A Collaborative Approach to Serving ELLs

SOURCE: Adapted from Glanz (2006).

The Practice of Collaborative Leadership

According to Rubin (2009), collaborative leaders help to create, build, manage, and sustain professional conversations among teachers, parents, community members, and labor organizers. Collaborative leaders are similar to transformational leaders who motivate people with a shared vision and mission or democratic leaders who involve stakeholders in the decision-making process, but they differ in that they do not make any major decisions on their own. Their main charge is to provide an environment that fosters group decision making, guide those efforts, and negotiate and resolve conflict.

A collaborative-leadership style is the optimal choice for those who wish to foster collaboration among their faculty, staff, and the greater school community. Conversely, school leaders cannot expect their community members to be collaborative under a top-down, do-as-I-say-but-not-as-I-do approach—it just won't work. You cannot create a collaborative school culture through bureaucratic command and control. Collaboration after all is a process—one that must be demonstrated, modeled, and guided into schoolwide practice.

With any leadership practice, there are various advantages and challenges in its application. Table 7.1 summarizes many of the benefits and demands of collaborative leadership. As you review this chart, consider some examples of these advantages and challenges as they manifest themselves in your own district. Reflect on how you and your team would work though the challenges and what strategies you would use to turn the advantages into actionable plans.

Table 7.1 Advantages and Challenges of Collaborative Leadership

Advantages	Challenges
• Advances stakeholder buy-in to the group's vision and mission • Increases individual responsibility and ownership • Enhances trust among group members • Provides a variety of perspectives • Reduces competition • Broadens the opportunity for success • Sustains leadership, assures stability and future commitment • Deepens people's willingness to find common ground • Creates a highly functioning organization	• Requires more time—to meet, share ideas, and come to consensus • Necessitates the ability to deal with disagreement and conflict—collaborative practices entail a great deal of give and take • Involves helping stakeholders ease their resistance to the collaborative process • Demands leaders to champion the group's goals and not their own • Calls for leaders to leave their egos "at the door"

SOURCE: Adapted from KU Work Group for Community Health and Development (2013).

Collaboration Lite or True Collaboration

In "'Collaboration Lite' Puts Students on a Starvation Diet," DuFour (2003) examined the different interpretations school leaders often have about what collaboration really means. He made the distinction between the routine activities, congenial teacher discourse, and social gatherings that are used as evidence of a collaborative culture—collaboration lite—with those that impact professional practices. Although many collegial efforts of teachers certainly are of great value, there is little evidence that these practices—being amiable, cooperative, and social—affect student achievement (Marzano, 2003). Table 7.2 outlines school practices that might be considered collaboration lite as compared with *true collaboration*—defined by DuFour (2003) as teacher teams focusing their collaborative conversations around three essential questions:

What is it we want our students to learn?

How do we know when each student has learned it?

How can we improve on current levels of student achievement? (p. 64)

DuFour (2003) cautioned, "True collaboration does not happen by chance or by invitation. It happens only when leaders commit to creating the systems that embed collaboration in the routine practices of the school" (p. 64).

The Leading Learner

In his work on the role of the building principal, Fullan (2014) highlighted key factors that increase a school leader's ability to amplify student

Table 7.2 Collaboration Lite Versus True Collaboration

Collaboration Lite	True Collaboration
• Congeniality and camaraderie • Discussing routine issues and procedures (e.g., discipline) • Willingness to work together; high levels of cooperation • Working on schoolwide committees and events	• Identifying results-oriented goals • Shifting focus from teacher input to student outcomes • Clarifying one's own and teacher teams' essential skills and knowledge • Analyzing one's own and teacher teams' strengths and weaknesses • Changing instructional practices through a collaborative process • Developing common assessments

learning. One aspect found to be most powerful in positively affecting student outcomes is the extent to which the school leader engages as a learner. In building a collaborative school culture, "The principal's role is to lead the school's teachers in a process of learning to improve their teaching, while learning alongside them about what works and what doesn't" (p. 55). As part of a framework to impact teacher learning, Fullan described how school leaders must "invest in capacity building with a focus on student results" (p. 67). He outlined his ideas for building what he calls professional capital as a framework for leading teacher learning. Hargreaves and Fullan (2013) explained professional capital in this way:

> It requires technical knowledge, high levels of education, strong practice within schools, and continuous improvement over time that is undertaken collaboratively, and that calls for the development of wise judgment. Over time, professional capital policies and practices build up the expertise of teachers individually and collectively to make a difference in the learning and achievement of all students. (p. 36)

More specifically, leading learners consider the development of knowledge and skills for continuous school improvement the responsibility of both school leaders and faculty. Through our research and work with school districts, we have witnessed some administrators who learn alongside their fellow teachers and others who leave the learning to the teachers themselves. Invariably, leaders who gain the same information, understanding, and expertise as their faculty have a greater success with guiding teacher practices and impacting student achievement. In addition, administrators who lead as learners help to eliminate fragmented instructional practices in favor of a systemic approach to school improvement through informed collaborative work.

TRANSFER TO PRACTICE

An abundance of diversity exists among those students who are identified as English learners. Part of this diversity stems from a great variation in the socioeconomic status of their families, their levels of academic achievement, parental or guardianship situation, and so on. These factors, among others, often lead educators to a deficit model of thinking—attributing students' lack of achievement to certain aspects of their cultures and communities. Yet closing the achievement gap for this student population calls for a movement away from deficit thinking and toward a model of collaborative learning among a wide range of school-community stakeholders.

BREAKING MENTAL MODELS AMONG STUDENTS, TEACHERS, AND THE COMMUNITY

Within a deficit model of thinking, the underachieving student is considered the problem. Bound by this way of thinking, "Schools are, at least in part, absolved from their responsibilities to educate all students appropriately, and this charge is shifted almost entirely to students and their families" (Irizarry, 2009, para.1). In identifying the problem in part, Colombo (2005) noted that this type of thinking could stem from a "cultural mismatch between teachers and the children they teach" (p. 1). For this reason, administrators, faculty, and staff must increase their understanding of diverse student populations. To further this cause, Colombo suggested professional learning initiatives focus on increasing empathy and decreasing misconceptions about different student populations and cultural groups among all stakeholders. Capper and Young (2014) emphasized the need to go even further and call for social justice leadership that creates "more inclusive/integrated and equitable communities, communities founded on respect and focused on providing full access and equitable outcomes" (p. 163).

A Leadership Voice From the Field

Dr. Margaret McKenzie, Coordinator, Office of ESOL (English for Speakers of Other Languages) and World Languages, Atlanta Public Schools, explains a change in leadership style:

> *The key to effective leadership for English learners requires a shift in mind-set from supervision to collaboration. It is only through the modeling and the creation of collaborative practices that we will cultivate a culture of inclusion and academic success for our English learners in our schools and in our districts.* (personal communication, July 23, 2014)

Advancing a Shared Belief

DuFour (2005) claimed,

Powerful collaboration . . . is a systematic process in which teachers work together to analyze and improve their classroom practice. Teachers work in teams, engaging in an ongoing cycle of questions that promote deep team learning. This process, in turn, leads to higher levels of student achievement. (p. 36)

In his essay "Masters of Motivation," Saphier (2005) offered a simple yet profound formula to help administrators establish a shared understanding of a critical belief. If you believe that teacher collaboration for the sake of ELLs is critical to your school's success, then consider undertaking the following actions:

- Say it
  - ○ Talk about it with conviction and passion but without stifling critical questions.

- Model it
  - ○ Show its importance by practicing collaboration with all faculty, including the ESL/ELD teachers.

- Organize it
  - ○ Create opportunities that value, encourage, and reward collaboration among faculty across disciplines and grades, especially for collaborative practices that serve ELLs.

- Protect it
  - ○ Stand behind teachers who exemplify collaboration despite difficulties by allocating resources such as collaborative time, technology tools, meeting space, and an abundance of encouragement.

- Reward it
  - ○ Recognize and celebrate teachers who practice collaboration for the sake of ELLs on a daily basis, both privately and publicly.

Developing and Sustaining a Collaborative School Culture

Who really decides what happens in the classroom, in a school, or in a district? Reeves (2006) noted that decision making may be best perceived on three levels within a school. Let's examine how such a model sheds light on supporting ELLs through the development of a collaborative school culture.

On Level 1, teachers make decisions individually and behind closed classroom doors. As such, teacher autonomy is reinforced. It is their discretion whether or not they will engage in collaborative practices. Each teacher may decide what type of collaboration and co-teaching practices he or she favors. Even when a co-teaching framework is in place, there are numerous choices to explore (for example, we offer seven possible co-teaching models in Chapter 4).

On Level 2, decisions are made collaboratively. Teachers and administrators identify and solve problems as a team. They agree on the type of collaborative model to employ (including the possibility of co-teaching) within the various ESL instructional-delivery models used in the building.

On Level 3, school administrators make sovereign decisions about issues that do not require collaborative decision making and fall outside the realm of teacher collaboration and co-teaching. Decisions regarding school safety and security fall into this level.

What defines a collaborative school culture for ELLs? We believe it is a culture in which a collective vision is developed, philosophical beliefs and values are shared, and a common purpose is articulated. In collaborative schools and districts, curricula are consistently aligned and revised to national, state, and local content and ESL standards. Teachers implement research-based instructional practices consistently across content areas and grade levels by sharing in the four phases of instruction: planning, teaching, assessing, and reflecting. Finally, effective frameworks are established and supported for ongoing professional learning that promotes teacher interaction and student inclusion that results in positive student outcomes and a socially just education for all. For a summary of key features of a collaborative school culture and their implications for English language learners, see Table 7.3.

Nurturing Teacher Leadership

Hoppey and McLeskey (2013) examined the role of the principal in the context of an effective inclusive school during the current era of high-stakes accountability. They found that the principal in the case study saw his role as "nurturing and caring for his staff, buffering his faculty from external pressures, associated with high-stakes accountability, providing high-quality professional development, and ensuring that teachers had opportunities to assume leadership roles in the school" (p. 245). The last finding—nurturing teacher leadership—contributes significantly to successful collaborative schools. Buchen (2000) argued,

> The only leadership that will make a difference is that of teachers. They alone are positioned where all the fulcrums are for change. They alone know what the day-to-day problems are and what it takes to solve them. They, not the principals, should be the ones to hire new teachers. They know what is needed. (p. 1)

Table 7.3 Features of a Collaborative School Culture

Feature	What It Is	What It Means for ELLs
Shared vision and mission	Clearly agreed-upon desired outcomes, shared values, and goals that focus on all students characterize the vision.	A culturally responsive school in which ELLs are not marginalized is the result.
Curriculum alignment	Through curriculum mapping and coordinated curriculum development programs, coherence is established.	Curriculum changes and modifications consider ELLs' linguistic and academic needs. ELLs are meaningfully included in general education curriculum learning.
Shared instructional practices	Planning, implementation, and assessment practices are coordinated among all faculty.	Differentiated instruction is designed and implemented with ELLs in mind.
Ongoing shared professional development	Individual teacher learning is integrated into collaborative efforts to enhance all teachers' practice.	All faculty interacting with ELLs understand and implement research-based methods for instructing and interacting with ELLs.
Student-centered approach	Instructional focus is on the needs of the learner; students develop their own understanding through active learning techniques.	ELLs are able to build their background knowledge and complete self-selected projects at their own level of linguistic ability.

We concur with Buchen's strong advocacy for teacher leadership and the sense of urgency it might bring about to develop teachers in various leadership roles. However, we further advocate for more opportunities in which teachers no longer feel they alone are in positions to make change and for schools in which both administrators and teachers use their particular expertise to guide the school community.

When teachers of ELLs develop a leadership role in the school community, they become the go-to people, get recognized for their expertise, and have a greater voice in shaping an integrated service delivery model of instruction for their students (Dove & Honigsfeld, 2010). As Whitaker, Whitaker, and Lumpa (2009) also observed, "To run a great school, it is essential to gain a full understanding of every teacher's unique abilities and passions. These in-house experts can be the 'go to' people available to anyone looking to improve their teaching techniques and themselves"

(p. 25). ESL/ELD teachers can also contribute to the embedded professional learning they receive through their participation in collaborative and co-taught classes. Furthermore, they can be strong voices in creating schoolwide collaborative practices for the sake of ELLs.

A Leadership Voice From the Field

Dr. Martina T. Wagner, Independent School District 623 English Language Supervisor, Roseville Area Schools, Minnesota, recognizes the importance of nurturing teacher leadership:

Collaboration among my co-teachers includes not only tried-and-true planning time, stellar instruction, and differentiation strategies but also the time that it takes to model co-teaching to those interested in trying it. Some of my most successful co-teachers began by seeing it happen down the hall . . . often wondering, How can I get that in my class? This often leads to peer observations that provide my curious and potential co-teachers an opportunity to learn to let go of control . . . by watching excellent co-teachers creating cultures within their classrooms where not only students but also co-teachers are encouraged and feel safe discussing learning, questioning one another, and therefore driving their own instruction.

Many of my co-teacher leaders are often sharing that at the end of the day the students should be tired but that they as teachers are not because they lean on each other. Co-teachers who lead and share their classrooms with their curious independently teaching colleagues create a culture where the reluctant feel encouraged to ask questions, start conversations, and make suggestions about potentially co-teaching while learning how collaboration will happen. One of my most memorable experiences as a leader of co-teaching teams was when I observed two co-teachers discussing their hopes for their partnership by stating, "I want to share what I know and to walk alongside you to learn, so that I can walk away having learned more than when I first started." (personal communication, August 22, 2014)

Assessing, Revising, and Maintaining Collaborative Service Delivery

We developed a comprehensive tool for assessing how collaborative your ESL service delivery is (see Box 7.1). Rate each dimension of the model on a Likert-type scale and identify the elements that received (a) the most outliers (extreme scores can indicate isolated cases that nonetheless deserve closer examination), (b) the lowest mean score (or lowest average score can suggest more systemic issues that need attention), and (c) the greatest variance of scores (all five levels selected by raters may indicate a lack of consensus or shared understanding about those elements).

Box 7.1 Assessing an Integrated, Collaborative Model to Serve Diverse Learners

Assessing an Integrated, Collaborative Model to Serve Diverse Learners

Rate the following activities on a scale of 1 to 5, with 1 indicating that it never takes place and 5 indicating that it is a most common practice.

1 = Never   2 = Rarely   3 = Sometimes   4 = Frequently   5 = Always or almost always

1. Interdisciplinary conversations
   a. to discuss students' academic, cognitive, and linguistic development   1 2 3 4 5
   b. to consider students' changing curricular and instructional needs and appropriate   1 2 3 4 5
      adaptations
   c. to explore extracurricular opportunities for diverse learners   1 2 3 4 5
   d. to examine student work   1 2 3 4 5
   e. to enhance parental involvement   1 2 3 4 5
Other:

2. Common planning opportunities
   a. to compare and align lesson objectives   1 2 3 4 5
   b. to design or modify instructional materials   1 2 3 4 5
   c. to adapt instructional strategies   1 2 3 4 5
   d. to adapt curriculum   1 2 3 4 5
   e. to align curriculum   1 2 3 4 5
   f. to engage in curriculum mapping   1 2 3 4 5
Other:

3. Shared classroom experiences
   a. classroom visits to observe each other's best practices   1 2 3 4 5
   b. classroom visits to observe student participation and learning in a range of 1 2 3 4 5
      instructional settings
   c. classroom visits to offer peer coaching   1 2 3 4 5
   d. co-teaching to deliver instruction collaboratively   1 2 3 4 5
Other:

4. Reflection and inquiry
   a. working in well-established teacher teams   1 2 3 4 5
   b. participating in collegial circles   1 2 3 4 5
   c. engaging in teacher study groups   1 2 3 4 5
   d. sharing professional readings (sharing literature on collaboration and ELD/ESL topics) 1 2 3 4 5
   e. conducting collaborative action research   1 2 3 4 5
   f. engaging in lesson study   1 2 3 4 5
   g. offering internal staff development for colleagues   1 2 3 4 5
Other:

5. Administrative support and feedback
   a. offering instructional leadership   1 2 3 4 5
   b. establishing logistical support for all levels of collaboration   1 2 3 4 5
   c. securing necessary materials and resources that support all learners   1 2 3 4 5
   d. offering ongoing professional development opportunities that foster collaboration 1 2 3 4 5
   e. creating a professional learning community   1 2 3 4 5
Other:

SOURCE: Adapted from Honigsfeld and Dove (2010a).

EXPANDING SHARED KNOWLEDGE AND COLLABORATIVE LEADERSHIP PRACTICES

The following resources and collaborative professional activities are designed to support your efforts as an administrator and instructional leader to build and expand a solid knowledge base about ELD/ESL programs and to develop collaborative-leadership practices.

Key Resources

Print Resources

- Causton, J., & Theoharis, G. (2014). *The principal's handbook for leading inclusive schools.* Baltimore, MD: Paul H. Brookes.
- Garmston, R. J., & Wellman, B. M. (2013). *The adaptive school: A sourcebook for developing collaborative groups.* Lanham, MD: Rowman and Littlefield.
- Glanz, J. G. (2006). *What every principal should know about collaborative leadership.* Thousand Oaks, CA: Corwin.
- Kruse, S. D., & Louis, K. S. (2009). *Building strong school cultures.* Thousand Oaks, CA: Corwin.

Online Resources

- California School Boards Association. (2009). *Building healthy communities: A school leader's guide to collaboration and community engagement.* Retrieved from http://www.csba.org/~/~/media/4D079093 73B14A0BB5CA2CCF41F98351.ashx

- Leithwood, K., Louis, K. S., Anderson, S., & Wahlstrom, K. (2004). *How leadership influences student learning.* Retrieved from http://www.wallacefoundation.org/knowledge-center/school-leadership/key-research/Documents/How-Leadership-Influences-Student-Learning.pdf

- Ohio Department of Education. (n.d.). *Ohio community collaboration model for school improvement: Implementation guide, version 2.* Retrieved from https://education.ohio.gov/getattachment/Topics/Other-Resources/Family-and-Community-Engagement/Models-for-Family-and-Community-Engagement/Collaboration-and-Collaborative-Leadership.pdf.aspx

- St. Paul Public Schools' Collaboration Lite and True Collaboration Nutrition Facts. Retrieved from http://mll.spps.org/uploads/ELL_Handbook_0809_Final.4.pdf

Activities for Professional Learning

1. Using the self-assessment tool presented in the outline for Integrated, Collaborative Model for ESL Services, evaluate the degree to which the ESL/ELD programs are implemented in a collaborative fashion twice a year. Create an action plan to set goals to advance to a more integrated, collaborative service delivery system.

2. Dr. Martina T. Wagner, ESL supervisor and consultant, who commented on her work regarding ELL teacher leadership earlier in this chapter, uses the following prompts to facilitate collaborative conversations with school and district leaders and teachers to support both the co-teaching initiative and ELL teacher leadership development.

   a. Do we have a clear and common vision?

   b. Are there incentives for the implementation of collaboration and co-teaching?

   c. Do key personnel possess the necessary knowledge and skills?

   d. Are adequate resources available?

   e. Has an action plan been developed? (personal communication, August 11, 2014)

Reflect on Dr. Wagner's guiding questions and decide how you would customize or augment them to best meet the needs at your own site.

3. We looked at Tung et al.'s (2011) study earlier. They found that leadership played a critical role in the success of consistently high-performing and dramatically improving schools for English language learners in Boston Public Schools. Among other factors, the authors emphasized that "teacher collaboration and expertise was the key to making high academic expectations of ELL students a reality" (p. 6). Additionally, it was also consistent among the four case study schools that

   when ELL students are in schools where the adults work collaboratively through structures that enhance professional community, ELL student achievement is high. If collaboration occurs among a racially and ethnically diverse staff that has an understanding of students' lives and cultures, in the study schools, student collaboration also crossed racial and ethnic lines in ways that promoted student learning. (p. 12)

Tung and her colleagues talk about structures that enhance professional community. Examine the current structures that are in place in your school that do that and develop an action plan to enhance them or design structures to create new opportunities for collaboration.

4. Todd Whitaker (2012) emphatically stated the following:

We can spend a great deal of time and energy looking for programs that will solve our problems, but these programs frequently do not bring the improvement or growth we seek. Instead we must focus on what really matters. It is never about programs, it is always about people. (p. 6)

As you finish reading this book, let's come to a full circle and think back to our discussion of ELLs in the first chapter: Who are all the members of your school community, and how do you make sure—through your leadership—that they know they matter?

References

Ainsworth, L. (2010). *Rigorous curriculum design: How to create curricular units of study that align standards, instruction, and assessment* [Kindle version].

Airasian, P. W., & Gullickson, A. (1994). Examination of teacher self-assessment. *Journal of Personnel Evaluation in Education, 8*(2), 195–203.

August, D., & Hakuta, K. (Eds.). (1998). *Educating language-minority children.* Washington, DC: National Academy Press.

Baker, K., & de Kanter, A. (Eds.). (1983). *Bilingual education: A reappraisal of federal policy.* Lexington, MA: Lexington Books.

Ballantyne, K. G., Sanderman, A. R., & Levy, J. (2008). *Educating English language learners: Building teacher capacity.* Washington, DC: National Clearinghouse for English Language Acquisition. Retrieved from http://www.ncela.gwu.edu/practice/mainstream_teachers.htm

Bhatia, T. K., & Ritchie, W. C. (Eds.). (2013). *The handbook of bilingualism and multi-lingualism* (2nd ed.). Malden, MA: Wiley-Blackwell.

Biemiller, A. (2003). Oral comprehension sets the ceiling on reading comprehension. *American Educator, 27*(1). Retrieved from https://www.aft.org/newspubs/periodicals/ae/spring2003/hirschsboral.cfm

Blankstein, A. M. (2013). *Failure is not an option: 6 principles that advance student achievement in highly effective schools.* Thousand Oaks, CA: Corwin.

Boyson, B. A., & Short, D. J. (2003). *Secondary school newcomer programs in the United States.* Washington, DC: Center for Applied Linguistics. Retrieved from http://www.cal.org/crede/pdfs/rr12.pdf

Breiseth, L. (2013). Getting to know your ELLs: Six steps for success. Retrieved from http://www.colorincolorado.org/article/59117.

Brisk, M. E. (2006). *Bilingual education: From compensatory to quality schooling.* Mahwah, NJ: Lawrence Earlbaum.

Buchen, I. H. (2000). The myth of school leadership. *Education Week, 19*(38), 1–3.

Calderón, M. E. (2007). *Teaching reading to English language learners, grades 6–12: A framework for improving achievement in the content areas.* Thousand Oaks, CA: Corwin.

Calderón, M. E., & Minaya-Rowe, L. (2003). *Designing and implementing two-way bilingual programs: A step-by-step guide for administrators, teachers, and parents.* Thousand Oaks, CA: Corwin.

Calderón, M. E., Slavin, R., & Sánchez, M. (2011). Effective instruction for English learners. *The Future of Our Children, 21*(1), 103–127.

California School Boards Association. (2009). *Building healthy communities: A school leader's guide to collaboration and community engagement.* Retrieved from http://www.csba.org/~/~/media/4D07909373B14A0BB5CA2CCF41F98351.ashx

Canady, R. L., & Rettig, M. D. (1995). The power of innovative scheduling. *Educational Leadership, 53*(3), 4–10.

Capper, C. A., & Frattura, E. (2009). *Meeting the needs of students of ALL abilities: How leaders go beyond inclusion* (2nd ed.). Thousand Oaks, CA: Corwin.

Capper, C. A., & Young, M. D. (2014). Ironies and limitations of educational leadership for social justice: A call to social justice educators. *Theory Into Practice, 53*(2), 158–164. doi: 10.1080/00405841.2014.885814

Causton, J., & Theoharis, G. (2014). *The principal's handbook for leading inclusive schools.* Baltimore, MD: Paul H. Brookes.

Cazden, C. B. (2001). *Classroom discourse: The language of teaching and learning* (2nd ed.). Portsmouth, NH: Heinemann.

Center for Collaborative Education. (2001). *Guide to collaborative culture and shared leadership.* Boston, MA: Author.

Chamot, A. U., & O'Malley, J. M. (1987). The cognitive academic language learning approach: A bridge to the mainstream. *TESOL Quarterly, 21,* 227–249.

Chamot, A. U., & O'Malley, J. M. (1994). *The CALLA handbook: Implementing the cognitive academic language learning approach.* Reading, MA: Addison-Wesley.

Chapman, C., & Hyatt, C. H. (2011). *Critical conversations in co-teaching: A problem-solving approach.* Bloomington, IN: Solution Tree.

Clark, K. (2009). The case for structured English immersion. *Educational Leadership, 66*(7), 42–46.

Cloud, N., Genesee, F., & Hamayan, E. (2000). *Dual language instruction: A handbook for enriched education.* Boston, MA: Heinle & Heinle.

Collier, V. P., & Thomas, W. P. (2004). The astounding effectiveness of dual language education for all. *NABE Journal of Research and Practice, 2*(1), 1–20.

Colombo, M. (2005). Reflections from teachers of culturally diverse students. *Beyond the Journal:* Young Children *on the Web.* Retrieved from https://www.naeyc.org/files/yc/file/200511/ColomboBTJ1105.pdf

Common Core State Standards for English Language Arts & Literacy in History/Social Studies, Science, and Technical Subjects (2010). Retrieved from http://corestandards.org/assets/CCSSI_ELA%20Standards.pdf

Crawford, J. (2008). *Advocating for English learners: Selected essays.* Clevedon, England: Multilingual Matters.

Daggett, W. R. (2012). Rigor/relevance framework. Retrieved from http://www.leadered.com/our-philosophy/rigor-relevance-framework.php

Danielson, C. (2007). The many faces of leadership. *Educational Leadership, 65*(1), 14–19.

Darling-Hammond, L., & Richardson. N. (2009). Teacher learning: What matters? *Educational Leadership, 66*(5), 46–53.

Deal, T. E., & Peterson, K. D. (1999). *Shaping school culture: The heart of leadership.* San Francisco, CA: Jossey-Bass.

DeCapua, A., Smathers, W., & Tang, L. F. (2007). Schooling, interrupted. *Educational Leadership, 64*(6), 40–46.

DeCapua, A., Smathers, W., & Tang, L. F. (2009). *Meeting the needs of students with limited or interrupted schooling: A guidebook for educators.* Ann Arbor: University of Michigan Press.

Dennis, T. (2014). Eight language program models: Four linguistic roads. *In-Sight: A Newsletter for Curriculum, Instruction, & Assessment.* Retrieved from http://www5.esc13.net/thescoop/insight/2014/03/eight-language-program-models-four-linguistic-roads/

Dove, M. G., & Colagiacomo, S. (2012). Instructional coaching and the content area teacher: Enhancing classroom practices. *Idiom, 42*(1), 22–23.

Dove, M. G., & Freeley, M. E. (2011). The effects of leadership on innovative program implementation. *The Delta Kappa Gamma Bulletin, 73*(3), 25–32.

Dove, M. G., & Honigsfeld, A. (2010). ESL co-teaching and collaboration: Opportunities to develop teacher leadership and enhance student learning. *TESOL Journal, 1*(1), 3–22.

Dove, M. G., & Honigsfeld, A. (2013). *Common core for the not-so-common learner, grades K–5: English language arts strategies.* Thousand Oaks, CA: Corwin.

Dove, M. G., & Honigsfeld, A. (2014). Analysis of the implementation of an ESL coteaching model in a suburban elementary school. *NYS TESOL Journal, 1*(1). 62–67.

Dove, M. G., Honigsfeld, A., & Cohan, A. (2014). *Beyond core expectations: A schoolwide framework for serving the not-so-common learner.* Thousand Oaks, CA: Corwin.

DuFour, R. (2003). "Collaboration lite" puts student achievement on a starvation diet. *Journal of Staff Development, 24*(4), 63–64.

DuFour, R. (2005). What is a professional learning community? In R. DuFour, R. Eaker, & R. DuFour (Eds.), *On common ground: The power of professional learning communities* (pp. 31–43). Bloomington, IN: Solution Tree.

DuFour, R. (2011). Working together: But only if you want to. *Phi Delta Kappan, 92*(5), 57–61.

Easton, L. (2008). Context: Establishing the environment for professional development. In L. Easton (Ed.), *Powerful designs for professional learning* (pp. 1–19). Oxford, England: The National Staff Development Council.

Echevarria, J., Vogt, M., & Short, D. J. (2008). *Making content comprehensible for English learners: The SIOP® model* (3rd ed.). Boston, MA: Pearson.

Echevarria, J., Vogt, M., & Short, D. J. (2010). *Making content comprehensible for elementary English learners: The SIOP® Model.* Boston, MA: Pearson.

Echevarria, J., Vogt, M., & Short, D. J. (2012). *Making content comprehensible for English learners: The SIOP® model* (4th ed.). Boston, MA: Pearson.

Elfers, A. M., & Stritikus, T. (2014). How school and district leaders support classroom teachers' work with English language learners. *Educational Administration Quarterly, 50,* 305–344. doi: 10.1177/0013161X13492797

Elmore, R. F. (2000). *Building a new structure for school leadership.* Retrieved from http://www.ashankerinst.org/Downloads/building.pdf

Erickson, H. L. (2006). *Concept-based curriculum and instruction for the thinking classroom.* Thousand Oaks, CA: Sage.

Esteban-Guitart, M., & Moll, L. C. (2014). Lived experience, funds of identity and education. *Culture & Psychology, 20,* 70–81. doi:10.1177/1354067X13515940

Fearon, K. (2008). *A team approach to ESL: An evaluative case study* (Master's thesis). Available from ProQuest Dissertations and Theses database. (UMI No. 1456437)

Ferguson, C. (2005). *Developing a collaborative team approach to support family and school connections with schools: What can school leaders do?* Retrieved from http://www.sedl.org/connections/resources/rb/research-brief3.pdf

Fisher, D., & Frey, N. (2007). *Checking for understanding: Formative assessment techniques for your classroom.* Alexandria, VA: Association for Supervision and Curriculum Development.

Fradd, S. H. (1998). Literacy development for language enriched pupils through English language arts instruction. In S. Fradd & O. Lee (Eds.), *Creating Florida's multilingual global work force: Educational policies and practices for students learning English as a new language* (pp. 47–56). Tallahassee: Florida Department of Education.

Frattura, E., & Capper, C. A. (2007). *Leading for social justice: Transforming schools for all learners.* Thousand Oaks, CA: Corwin.

Freeman, D. E., & Freeman, Y. S. (1988). *Sheltered English instruction* (ERIC Document Reproduction Service No. ED301070). Retrieved from http://thememoryhole.org/edu/eric/ed301070.html

Freeman, Y. S., & Freeman, D. E. (with Mercuri, S.). (2002). *Closing the achievement gap: How to reach limited-formal-schooling and long-term English learners.* Portsmouth, NH: Heinemann.

Frey, N., Fisher, D., & Nelson, J. (2013). Todo tiene que ver con lo que se habla: It's all about the talk. *Kappan, 94*(6), 8–13.

Friend, M., & Cook, L. (2012). *Interactions: Collaboration skills for school professionals.* Boston, MA: Allyn & Bacon.

Fullan, M. (2007). *The new meaning of educational change* (4th ed.). New York: Teachers College Press.

Fullan, M. (2011). *Choosing the wrong drivers for whole system reform* (Centre for Strategic Education Seminar Series Paper No. 204). Retrieved from http://theeta.org/wp-content/uploads/2011/11/eta-articles-110711.pdf

Fullan, M. (2014). *The principal: Three keys to maximizing impact.* San Francisco, CA: Jossey-Bass.

Gajda, R., & Koliba, C. J. (2008). Evaluating and improving the quality of teacher collaboration: A field-tested framework for secondary school leaders. *NASSP Bulletin, 92*(2), 133–153.

Garmston, R. J., & Wellman, B. M. (2013). *The adaptive school: A sourcebook for developing collaborative groups.* Lanham, MD: Rowman and Littlefield.

Genesee, F., Lindholm-Leary, K., Saunders, W., & Christian, D. (2005). English language learners in U.S. schools: An overview of research findings. *Journal of Education for Students Placed at Risk, 10*(4), 363–385.

Glanz, J. (2006). *What every principal should know about collaborative leadership.* Thousand Oaks, CA: Corwin.

Glatthorn, A. A., Boschee, F., & Whitehead, B. M. (2006). *Curriculum leadership: Development and implementation.* Thousand Oaks, CA: Sage.

Goodlad, J. I, Mantle-Bromley, C., & Goodlad, S. J. (2004). *Education for everyone: Agenda for education in a democracy.* San Francisco, CA: Jossey-Bass.

Gottlieb, M. (2006). *Assessing English language learners: Bridges from language proficiency to academic achievement.* Thousand Oaks, CA: Corwin.

Gottlieb, M., & Ernst-Slavin, G. (2014). *Academic language in diverse classrooms: Definitions and contexts.* Thousand Oaks, CA: Corwin.

Guskey, T. R. (2014). *On your mark: Challenging the conventions of grading and reporting.* Bloomington, IN: Solution Tree.

Guskey, T. R., & Jung, L. A. (2013). *Answers to essential questions about standards, assessments, grading, and reporting.* Thousand Oaks, CA: Corwin.

Hamayan, E., Genesee, F., & Cloud, N. (2013). *Dual language instruction from A to Z: Practical guidance for teachers and administrators.* Portsmouth, NH: Heinemann.

Hargreaves, A., & Fullan, M. (2013). The power of professional capital. *Journal of Staff Development, 34*(3), 36–39. Retrieved from http://www.michaelfullan.ca/wp-content/uploads/2013/08/JSD-Power-of-Professional-Capital.pdf

Hattie, J. (2012). *Visible learning for teachers.* New York, NY: Routledge.

Hauck, M. C., Wolf, M. K., & Mislevy, R. J. (2013). *Creating a next-generation system of K-12 English learner (EL) language proficiency assessments.* Retrieved from http://www.ets.org/research/policy_research_reports/publications/paper/2013/jrld

Haynes, J., & Zacarian, D. (2010). *Teaching English language learners across the content areas.* Alexandria, VA: Association for Supervision and Curriculum Development.

Hern, K. (with Snell, M.). (2013). *Toward a vision of accelerated curriculum & pedagogy.* Retrieved from http://www.learningworksca.org/wp-content/uploads/2012/02/AcceleratingCurriculum_508.pdf

Hirsh, S. (2009). Before deciding what to do, determine what is necessary. *Journal of Staff Development, 30*(1), 71–72.

Hirsh, S., & Killion, J. (2009). When educators learn, students learn: Eight principles of professional learning. *Phi Delta Kappan, 90*(7), 464–469.

Honigsfeld, A., & Dove, M. (2008). Co-teaching in the ESL Classroom. *The Delta Kappa Gamma Bulletin, 74*(2), 8–14.

Honigsfeld, A., & Dove, M. G. (2010a). *Collaboration and co-teaching: Strategies for English learners.* Thousand Oaks, CA: Corwin.

Honigsfeld, A., & Dove, M. (2010b). Co-teaching 201: How to support ELLs. *New Teacher Advocate, 17*(3), 4–5.

Honigsfeld, A., & Dove, M. G. (Eds.). (2012a). *Coteaching and other collaborative practices in the EFL/ESL classroom: Rationale, research, reflections, and recommendations.* Charlotte, NC: Information Age.

Honigsfeld, A., & Dove, M. G. (2012b). Collaborative practices to support English learners. *Principal Leadership, 12*(5), 40–44.

Honigsfeld, A., & Dove, M. G. (2013). *Common Core for the not-so-common learner, grades 6–12: English language arts strategies.* Thousand Oaks, CA: Corwin.

Hoppey, D., & McLeskey, J. (2013). A case study of principal leadership in an effective inclusive school. *Journal of Special Education, 46*(4), 245–256.

Howard, E. R., & Sugarman, J. (2001). *Two-way immersion programs: Features and statistics.* Retrieved from http://www.cal.org/resources/digest/0101twi.html

Howard, L., &. Potts, E. A. (2009). Using co-planning time: Strategies for a successful coteaching marriage. *TEACHING Exceptional Children Plus, 5*(4). Retrieved from http://journals.cec.sped.org/tecplus/vol5/iss4/art2/

Irizarry, J. (2009). Cultural deficit model. Retrieved from http://www.education.com/reference/article/cultural-deficit-model/

Jacobs, H. H. (1997). *Mapping the big picture: Integrating curriculum and assessment K–12.* Alexandria, VA: Association for Supervision and Curriculum Development.

Jacobs, H. H. (2010). Upgrading the curriculum: 21st century assessment types and skills. In H. H. Jacobs (Ed.), *21st century curriculum: Essential education for a changing world* (pp. 18–29). Alexandria, VA: Association for Supervision and Curriculum Development.

Johnson, C., & Marx, S. (2009). Transformative professional development: A model for urban science education reform. *Journal of Science Teacher Education, 20*(2), 113–134. doi:10.1007/s10972–009–9127-x

Joyce, B. R., & Calhoun, E. (2010). *Models of professional development: A celebration of educators.* Thousand Oaks, CA: Corwin.

Jung, L. A., & Guskey, T. R. (2012). *Grading exceptional and struggling learners.* Thousand Oaks, CA: Corwin.

Katzenmeyer, M. H., & Moller, G. V. (2001). *Awakening the sleeping giant: Helping teachers develop as leaders* (2nd ed.). Thousand Oaks, CA: Corwin.

Kinsella, K. (2012). Cutting to the core: Communicating on the same wavelength. *Language Magazine, 12*(4), 18–25.

Kohm, B., & Nance, B. (2009). Creating collaborative cultures. *Educational Leadership, 67*(2), 67–72.

Kruse, S. D., & Louis, K. S. (2009). *Building strong school cultures.* Thousand Oaks, CA: Corwin.

KU Work Group for Community Health and Development. (2013). *Collaborative Leadership.* Retrieved from http://ctb.ku.edu/en/table-of-contents/leadership/leadership-ideas/collaborative-leadership/main

Langer, G. M., Colton, A. B., & Gott, L. S. (2003). *Collaborative analysis of student work: Improving teaching and learning.* Alexandria, VA: Association for Supervision and Curriculum Development.

Langer de Ramirez, L. (2009). *Empower English language learners with tools from the web.* Thousand Oaks, CA: Corwin.

Learning Forward (2011). Standards of professional learning. Retrieved from http://learningforward.org/standards

Leithwood, K., Louis, K. S., Anderson, S., & Wahlstrom, K. (2004). *How leadership influences student learning.* Retrieved from http://www.wallacefoundation.org/knowledge-center/school-leadership/key-research/Documents/How-Leadership-Influences-Student-Learning.pdf

Linquanti, R., & Cook, H. G. (2013). *Toward a "common definition of English learner": Guidance for states and state assessment consortia in defining and addressing policy and technical issues and options.* Retrieved from http://www.ccsso.org/Documents/2013/Toward_a_Common_Definition_2013.pdf

López, F., & Iribaren, J. (2014). Creating and sustaining inclusive instructional settings for English language learners: Why, what, and how. *Theory Into Practice, 53,* 106–114. doi: 10.1080/00405841.2014.885810

Ma, J. (2002). *What works for children: What we know and don't know about bilingual education.* Boston, MA: Harvard University Press.

Martinez-Wenzl, M., Perez, K., & Gandara, P. (2012). Is Arizona's approach to educating its ELs superior to other forms of instruction? *Teachers College Record, 114*(9), 1–32.

Marzano, R. J. (2003). *What works in schools: Translating research into action.* Alexandria, VA: Association for Supervision and Curriculum Development.

Marzano, R. J., Waters, T., & McNulty, B. A. (2005). *School leadership that works: From research to results.* Alexandria, VA: Association for Supervision and Curriculum Development; Aurora, CO: Mid-continent Research for Education and Learning.

May, S. (2008). Bilingual/immersion education: What the research tells us. In J. Cummins & N. H. Hornberger (Eds.), *Encyclopedia of language and education* (2nd ed., Vol. Bilingual Education, pp. 19–34). New York, NY: Springer.

McLaughlin, B., & McLeod, B. (1996). *Educating all our students: Improving education for children from culturally and linguistically diverse backgrounds*. Santa Cruz, CA: National Center for Research on Cultural Diversity and Second Language Learning.

McLaughlin, M.W., & Talbert, J. E. (2006). *Building school-based teacher learning communities: Professional strategies to improve student achievement*. New York, NY: Teachers College Press.

Moll, L. C., Amanti, C., Neff, D., & Gonzalez, N. (1992). Funds of knowledge for teaching: Using a qualitative approach to connect homes and classrooms. *Theory Into Practice, 21*, 132–141.

Muhammad, A. (2009). *Transforming school culture: How to overcome staff division*. Bloomington, IN: Solution Tree.

Murawski, W. W. (2005). *Co-teaching in the inclusive classroom: Working together to help all your students find success*. Bellevue, WA: Bureau of Education and Research.

Murawski, W. W., & Dieker, L. (2008). 50 ways to keep your co-teacher: Strategies for before, during and after co-teaching. *TEACHING Exceptional Children, 40*, 40–48.

Nieto, S. (2009). From surviving to thriving. *Educational Leadership, 66*(5), 8–13.

The No Child Left Behind Act of 2001, 20 U.S.C. 6301 (2002). Retrieved from http://www.ed.gov/nclb/landing.jhtml

Nye, K., & Capelluti, J. (2003). The ABCS of decision making. *Principal Leadership, 3*(9), 8–9. Retrieved from http://www.nassp.org/Portals/0/Content/46883.pdf

Oblakor, F. E., & Yawn, C. D. (2013). Reducing achievement gaps and increasing the school success of culturally and linguistically diverse students with special needs using the comprehensive support model. In C. M. Wilson & S. D. Horsford (Eds.). *Advancing equity and achievement in America's diverse schools: Inclusive theories, policies, and practices* (pp. 159–170). New York, NY: Routledge.

Ohio Department of Education. (n.d.). *Ohio community collaboration model for school improvement: Implementation guide, version 2*. Retrieved from https://education.ohio.gov/getattachment/Topics/Other-Resources/Family-and-Community-Engagement/Models-for-Family-and-Community-Engagement/Collaboration-and-Collaborative-Leadership.pdf.aspx

Olsen, L., & Jaramillo, A. (1999). *Turning the tides of exclusion: A guide for educators and advocates for immigrant students*. Oakland, CA: The California Tomorrow.

O'Malley, J. M., & Valdez Pierce, L. (1996). *Authentic assessment for English language learners: Practical approaches for teachers*. Reading, MA: Addison-Wesley.

Osterman, K. F., & Kottkamp, R. B. (2004). *Reflective practice for educators: Professional development to improve student learning* (2nd ed.). Thousand Oaks, CA: Corwin.

Pappamihiel, N. E. (2012). Benefits and challenges of co-teaching English learners in one elementary school in transition. *The Tapestry Journal, 4*(1), 1–13.

Paulu, N., & Winters, K. (1998). *Teachers leading the way*. Washington, DC: U.S. Department of Education.

Peterson, K. (with R. Brietzke). (1994). *Building collaborative cultures: Seeking ways to reshape urban schools*. Retrieved from http://www.ncrel.org/sdrs/areas/issues/educatrs/leadrshp/le0pet.htm

Piercey, D. (2010). Why don't teachers collaborate? A leadership conundrum. *Phi Delta Kappan, 92*(1), 54–56.

Rance-Roney, J. (2009). Best practices for adolescent ELLs. *Educational Leadership, 66*(7), 32–37.

Reeves, D. (2006). *The learning leader: How to focus school improvement for better results.* Alexandria, VA: Association for Supervision and Curriculum Development.

Rivera, M., Francis, D. J., Fernandez, M., Moughamian, A. C., Lesaux, N., & Jergensen, J. (2010). *Effective practices for English language learners: Principals from five states speak.* Portsmouth, NH: RMC Research Corporation, Center on Instruction. Retrieved from http://eric.ed.gov/?id=ED517795

Rollins, P. S. (2014). *Learning in the fast lane: 8 ways to put ALL students on the road to academic success.* Alexandria, VA: Association for Supervision and Curriculum Development.

Rothenberg, C., & Fisher, D. (2007). *Teaching English language learners: A differentiated approach.* Upper Saddle River, NJ: Pearson.

Rubin, H. (2009). *Collaborative leadership: Developing effective partnerships for communities and schools.* Thousand Oaks, CA: Corwin.

Ryan, C. (2013). *Language use in the United States: 2011.* Washington, DC: U.S. Census Bureau. Retrieved from http://www.census.gov/prod/2013pubs/acs-22.pdf

Sacks, L. (2014, June 17). It's not enough to talk the talk [Web log post]. Retrieved from http://blogs.edweek.org/edweek/learning_deeply/2014/06/its_not_enough_to_talk_the_talk.html

Saide, B., & Fox Sr., J. (2014, July 10). Reflect or refract: Top 3 tips for the reflective educator [Web log post]. Retrieved from http://www.wholechildeducation.org/blog/reflect-or-refract

Saphier, J. (2005). Masters of motivation. In R. DuFour, R. Eaker, & R. DuFour (Eds.), *On common ground: The power of professional learning communities* (pp. 105–109). Bloomington, IN: Solution Tree.

Scanlan, M., Frattura, E., Schneider, K., & Capper, C. (2012). Bilingual students within integrated comprehensive services: Collaborative strategies. In A. Honigsfeld & M. G. Dove (Eds.), *Coteaching and other collaborative practices in the EFL/ESL classroom: Rationale, research, reflections, and recommendations* (pp. 3–13). Charlotte, NC: Information Age.

Scanlan, M., & Lopez, F. (2012). ¡Vamos! How school leaders promote equity and excellence for bilingual students. *Educational Administration Quarterly, 48*(4), 583–625. doi:10.1177/0013161X11436270

Schatz, M., & Wilkinson, L. C. (Eds.). (2010). *The education of English language learners: Research to practice.* New York, NY: Guilford Press.

Schon, D. E. (1990). *Educating the reflective practitioner: Toward a new design for teaching and learning in the professions.* San Francisco, CA: Jossey-Bass.

Sergiovanni, T. J. (2000). *The lifeworld of leadership: Creating culture, community, and personal meaning in our schools.* San Francisco, CA: Jossey-Bass.

Simone, J. (2012). *Addressing the marginalized student: The secondary principal's role in eliminating deficit thinking* (Doctoral dissertation). Retrieved from https://www.ideals.illinois.edu/handle/2142/31100

Smith, D., Wilson, B., & Corbett, D. (2009). Moving beyond talk. *Educational Leadership, 66*(5), 20–25.

Sparks, D. (2005). *Leading for results: Teaching, learning, and relationships in schools.* Thousand Oaks, CA: Corwin.

Sparks, D., & Hirsh, S. (1997). *A new vision for staff development*. Alexandria, VA: Association for Supervision and Curriculum Development.

Staehr Fenner, D. (2013a). *Advocating for English learners: A guide for educators*. Thousand Oaks, CA: Corwin.

Staehr Fenner, D. (2013b). *Implementing the Common Core State Standards for English learners: The changing role of the ESL teacher*. Retrieved from http://www.tesol .org/docs/default-source/advocacy/ccss_convening_final-5-7-13.pdf?sfvrsn=8

Stanford University. (2013). *Key principles for ELL instruction*. Retrieved from http://ell.stanford.edu/sites/default/files/Key%20Principles%20for%20 ELL%20Instruction%20with%20references_0.pdf

Stetson, F. (2014). *Finding time for collaboration and using it well*. Retrieved from http://inclusiveschools.org/finding-time-for-collaboration-and-using-it-well/

Stronge, J. H., Richard, H. B., & Catano, N. (2008). *Qualities of effective principals*. Alexandria, VA: Association for Supervision and Curriculum Development.

Tallerico, M. (2005). *Supporting and sustaining teachers' professional development: A principal's guide*. Thousand Oaks, CA: Corwin.

Teachers of English to Speakers of Other Languages. (2006). *TESOL PreK–12 English language proficiency standards*. Alexandria, VA: Author.

Theoharis, G. (2009). *The school leaders our children deserve: Seven keys to equity, social justice, and school reform*. New York, NY: Teachers College Press.

Theoharis, G., & O'Toole, J. (2011). Leading inclusive ELL: Social justice leadership for English language learners. *Educational Administration Quarterly 47*(4), 646–688. doi: 10.1177/0013161X11401616

Thomas, W. P., & Collier, V. P. (2002). *A national study of school effectiveness for language minority students' long-term academic achievement* (Project 1.1). Washington, DC: Center for Research on Education, Diversity & Excellence.

Tung, R., Uriarte, M., Diez, V., Gagnon, L., & Stazesky, P., with de los Reyes, E., & Bolomey, A. (2011). *Learning from consistently high performing and improving schools for English language learners in Boston Public Schools*. Boston, MA: Center for Collaborative Education. Retrieved from http://files.eric.ed.gov/fulltext/ ED540998.pdf

Udelhofen, S. (2005). *Keys to curriculum mapping: Strategies and tools to make it work*. Thousand Oaks, CA: Corwin.

U.S. Department of Education, Office of Elementary and Secondary Education. (2007). *Assessment and accountability for recently arrived and former limited English proficient (LEP) students*. Retrieved from www.ed.gov/policy/elsec/ guid/lepguidance.doc

Valdés, G., Kibler, A., & Walqui, A. (2014). *Changes in the expertise of ESL professionals: Knowledge and action in an era of new standards*. Retrieved from http:// www.tesol.org/docs/default-source/papers-and-briefs/professional-paper-26-march-2014.pdf?sfvrsn=2

Villa, R., & Thousand, J. (Eds.). (2005). *Creating an inclusive school*. Alexandria, VA: Association for Supervision and Curriculum Development.

Villa, R. A., Thousand, J. S., & Nevin, A. I. (2013). *A guide to co-teaching: New lessons and strategies to facilitate student learning* (3rd ed.). Thousand Oaks, CA: Corwin.

Virginia Institute for Developmental Disabilities. (2001). *Creating collaborative IEPs: A handbook*. Richmond: Author.

Waff, D. (2009). Coresearching and coreflecting: The power of teacher inquiry communities. In D. Goswami, C. Lewis, M. Rutherford, & D. Waff (Eds.), *Teacher inquiry: Approaches to language and literacy research* (pp. 69–89). New York, NY: Teachers College Press.

Walqui, A., & van Lier, L. (2010). *Scaffolding the academic success of adolescent English language leaners: A pedagogy of promise.* San Francisco, CA: WestEd.

Wertheimer, C., & Honigsfeld, A. (2000). Preparing ESL students to meet the new standards. *TESOL Journal, 9*(1), 23–28.

Whitaker, T. (2012). *What great principals do differently: Eighteen things that matter most* (2nd ed.). New York, NY: Routledge.

Whitaker, T., Whitaker, B., & Lumpa, D. (2009). *Motivating and inspiring teachers: The educational leader's guide for building staff morale.* New York, NY: Routledge.

Wiggins, G., & McTighe, J. (2005). *Understanding by design* (2nd ed.). Alexandria, VA: Association for Supervision and Curriculum Development.

World-Class Instructional Design and Assessment Consortium. (2007). *2007 English language development standards: Kindergarten–Grade 12.* Retrieved from http://www.wida.us/standards/eld.aspx

World-Class Instructional Design and Assessment Consortium. (2012). *2012 amplification of the English language development standards: Kindergarten–Grade 12.* Retrieved from http://www.wida.us/downloadLibrary.aspx

World-Class Instructional Design and Assessment Consortium. (2014). *The WIDA standards framework and its theoretical foundations.* Retrieved from http://wida.us/DownloadDocs/standards/TheoreticalFramework.pdf

York-Barr, J., Sommers, W. A., Ghere, G. S., & Montie, J. (2006). *Reflective practice to improve schools: An action guide for educators.* Thousand Oaks, CA: Corwin.

Zacarian, D. (2013). *Mastering academic language.* Thousand Oaks, CA: Corwin.

Zehr, M. A. (2006, December 5). Team-teaching helps close the language gap. *Education Week*, pp. 26–29. Retrieved from http://www.edweek.org/ew/articles/2006/12/06/14hmong.h26.html

Zigler, E., & Weiss, H. (1985). Family support systems: An ecological approach to child development. In R. N. Rapoport (Ed.), *Children, youth, and families: The action-research relationship* (pp. 166–205). Cambridge, England: Cambridge University Press.

Zwiers, J. (2014). *Building academic language: Meeting Common Core Standards across disciplines, Grades 5–12* (2nd ed.). San Francisco, CA: Jossey-Bass.

Index

A SAGE Company

Corwin is committed to improving education for all learners by publishing books and other professional development resources for those serving the field of PreK–12 education. By providing practical, hands-on materials, Corwin continues to carry out the promise of its motto: **"Helping Educators Do Their Work Better."**